GIST OF ART

GIST OF ART

BY

JOHN SLOAN

Principles and Practise expounded in the Classroom and

Studio, recorded with the assistance of HELEN FARR

AMERICAN ARTISTS GROUP, INC., NEW YORK

GIST OF ART

COPYRIGHT, 1939, BY

AMERICAN ARTISTS GROUP, INC.

DESIGNED BY A. A. VERSH

TO

AMELIA ELIZABETH WHITE

AND

DOLLY SLOAN
*The little woman who has been
my right hand man*

IN APPRECIATION

My Sincere Thanks are hereby extended to friends and former students whose notes and correspondence have been of material assistance in the preparation of this book. To Minette Barton, A. S. Baylinson, Virginia Beach, Jules Billington, Virginia Butler, John Cunningham, Thomas Donnelly, Don Freeman, Fred Gardner, Esther Goetz, John Gregory, Virginia Gresham, Isabel Hamilton, Harry Hering, Marion Humfeld, Jeanette Jamison, A. F. Levinson, Holt McAloney, Joseph Pollet, Mrs. Frances Seckler Reswick, Aline Rhonie, Doris Rosenthal, Janice Sandler, Mrs. Leon Semenoff, Fred Shane, Clara Skinner, Jenny Slaughter, John Stark, Thomas Stevens, Beulah Stevenson, Ethel Swantees, and Kay von Minckwitz.

J. S.

PUBLISHER'S NOTE

Every great movement of human endeavor requires a parallel literature—to record, to interpret, to transmit. This is true of science, of the events we call history, of literature itself and likewise of art.

The works of an artist do not emanate from his hands and eyes alone as though these organs were self-operating instruments, like a camera.

Art in its making has a biology; and no less does it have its philosophy as well. Poetry, too, accompanies art inevitably; and in addition to the technique of art, comprising the study and evolution of methods as such, there are also aspects of the sciences—physics, chemistry, optics.

Together, these constitute the living forces of art—vast, heterogeneous, individual. To render these forces for each important American artist adequately, authoritatively, would be to turn a whole series of illuminating lanterns upon his real, interior genius—a light in which his life and his work would be more precisely, more abundantly understood and appreciated; not alone for the guidance of those who make pictures but as well for the benefit of those who look at pictures.

Too often have the lives and teachings of our great artists been left for their recording and interpretation to subsequent generations—to be reconstructed somehow, at farthest remove from every living source.

The American Artists Group now undertakes to correct this condition by dedicating itself to the building—book by book, artist by artist—of an authoritative parallel literature of contemporary American art; to round out, to enrich the contributions which the important artists of the present day are making.

The conviction still persists that it is not wise to undertake an appraisal of an artist's work during his lifetime; that the authoritative book about him had best be deferred until after his death. However, it seems highly important that the artist be given the opportunity of recording his convictions; even though his opinions in relation to his own experiences and his own work may prove faulty to a degree and may not be borne out by future evaluations.

The creation of this library is no accident or caprice. It originates from a need—actual, vital, measurable. Among other varied activities which it has pursued since its organization in 1935, the American Artists Group has conducted traveling art exhibitions in hundreds of communities. The itineraries of these exhibits have reached every section of the country—cities, towns and villages. From this nation-wide contact, the Group has come face to face with America's artistic awakening in its most compelling reality.

The books to be published in this series will be as comprehensive as it is possible for the publisher and the artist to make them. The authors of the various books will, wherever possible, be the artists themselves. Where this is not feasible, the author will be one whose qualifications will insure an intimate and definitive portrayal.

Each book will be fully illustrated with reproductions of the artist's work from his beginnings on through maturity.

In this the first volume, the publishers offer a foretaste of a series which is designed to become an invaluable concurrent record of those distinguished artists who by their lives and achievements are contributing to a genuinely native American Renaissance.

CONTENTS

ILLUSTRATIONS

GIST OF ART

CHAPTER I

POINT OF VIEW ABOUT LIFE

FROM TIME TO TIME I have been asked for a biography, but there there has been nothing eventful in my life. There have been ups and downs, but the main thing about it has been my work. What more do you want to know about an artist when you have his work? Even Giotto and Rembrandt were just simple men. There is very little known about Shakespeare. He was so simple they didn't notice him.

Here, therefore, is not a biography. It is merely a record of the thoughts and impulses that have been behind my work and teaching. It might be well, however, to start out with some of the beginnings of my rather tame career—the early influences.

My father was an artist, a skillful craftsman, painting in his spare time. A total wreck in business. My mother a humorful, gentle lady. My sisters and I all drew equally well.

Back in the Nineties, when I was working for the *Philadelphia Inquirer*, I met Beisen Kubota, Japanese Art Commissioner to the Chicago World's Fair, and I began drawing in a flat, sort of Japanese, black and white style. I was given recognition as one of the "poster movement." That was before I had ever seen the work of Beardsley, McCarter, Bradley, Steinlen, and Toulouse-Lautrec.

It was Robert Henri who brought me some Daumier lithographs and also a set of Goya's aquatints. Boardman Robinson's illustrations in the Sunday New York *Morning Telegraph* were a great inspiration. Steinlen in *Le Rire* was great in those days, so was Forain. Turner was another early influence.

At that time news illustrations were pen and ink drawings made from photographs or sketches made on the spot. The half-tone process had not yet been adapted to newspaper print. The staff artists were sent out to cover fires, parades, elections, and other happenings. Later, the staff photographer would bring in prints for us to work from. If the drawing had to be made in a hurry, the photograph would be cut up in sections and several artists would work on the drawings.

We studied the work of the English line draughtsmen: Leech, Keene, *et al*, men who worked for *Punch* and the newspapers. There was also Constantin Guys. These men usually made pencil or pen drawings directly on the block; or their drawings were photographed on the block. It was the engraver's job to cut the block.

About thirty years ago a critic called me "the American Hogarth." The idea stuck. You know how writers look up old articles when they are going to write something? I wish that remark were more true. I rate Hogarth as the greatest English artist who ever lived. He was certainly greater than Reynolds. And who else is there besides Constable? Of course, there is Blake, but one doesn't think of him as a painter.

Hogarth painted the life around him, with an illustrator's point of view, a very healthy thing for an artist. He was able to develop a sort of system in drawing and composition. He found a kind of beauty in life through his interest in real character. His engraved plates are powerful in plastic design and so full of humanity. The paintings made in the same vein are very great, but they say that when he tried to paint in the grand historical manner the work went up a tree. As for *The Fish Girl* so much admired by connoisseurs, I think he tossed that off to show that he knew how to make a flashy painting. His real things seem to be underpainted and glazed in the traditional formal technique.

One or two of the heads I painted in Philadelphia, back in those

JOHN SLOAN in 1897 when he was a
staff artist on the Philadelphia 'Press'.

JOHN SLOAN *at the time the Addison Gallery of the Phillips Academy, Andover, Massachusetts, presented a retrospective exhibition of his paintings, drawings and prints.*

early days, look like the work of Frans Hals. I wonder if I would have come to a consciousness of the plastic concept by following in that direction? I came to it by working from memory and through the influence of the ultra-modern movement.

It was Robert Henri who set me to painting seriously; without his inspiring friendship and guidance I probably might never have thought of it at all. At that time I painted with a dark palette and denied the existence of blue effects, atmosphere, the whole theory of impressionism. My subjects were chosen with an illustrative point of view, literary, poetic motives. When an incident impressed me very much I wanted to make a painting of it. Today, any old subject will do. The model comes into the studio and takes a pose, and I start to paint. There are not so many finished pictures, now, but there is more study. Only now and then I start with pictorial intent.

When I came to New York in 1905 and was dependent on magazine and book illustrations for a living, I never could paint until I had an order for a job in my desk. Then I would paint day and night until the last moment and do the drawings just in time to make the dead-line. I have always been that way. I can't work when I am worried about the rent.

There is so much talk today about the American Scene. As though it had been discovered in the last decade! If anyone started this painting of the American scene it was our gang of newspaper men: Glackens, Luks, Shinn, and myself, back in the Nineties. But we didn't really start it. What about Homer, Eakins, and lesser men?

There is also much talk today about socially-conscious painting. My old work was unconsciously very much so, especially before I became a Socialist. After that I felt that such a thing should not be put into painting and I reserved it for my etching. They may say that I am now fiddling while Rome burns, but I question whether social propaganda is necessary to the life of a work of art.

I don't see how a thoughtful artist under a Fascist or Communist government, where free expression is heresy, could help wanting to express his social feelings in his work. In this relatively democratic country today, I feel that, since we can talk about things freely, we can go on painting any kind of subject matter we like.

It is not necessary to paint the American flag to be an American painter. As though you didn't see the American scene whenever you open your eyes! I am not for the American scene, I am for mental realization. If you are American and work, your work will be American.

Patriotism, love of country, is very different from love for the government. I love the country in Pennsylvania, New England, and in the Southwest. I love the streets of New York. But I am suspicious of all government because government is violence. In the United States you must not speak for Communism. In Russia you cannot speak against it. Communism is government by the people, but the trouble is that so many people are the Fido type. In America the country is run by about a hundred bosses. In Russia and Germany there is one boss for every twenty men. There are more bosses but that is not freedom.

The governments are willing to turn their weapons, and tear bombs are the least of them, against the enemy or against their own people, their own citizens. Young people in their twenties are going to see things that I would like to live to see and yet it won't be pleasant. It will be terrible.

I don't like war. The economic interests get out their propaganda machines and persuade the people that democracy is at stake. And what do millions of innocent people go out and get killed and maimed for?—to protect the economic interests of the few.

Ever since the Great War broke out in 1914 this world has been a crazy place to live in. I hate war and I put that hatred into

[4]

cartoons in the (old) *Masses*. But I didn't go sentimental and paint pictures of war. I went on painting and etching the things I saw around me in the city streets and on the roof tops.

War, blood, hate; poison gases; shell-shocked, mangled men; the competitive spirit—that is what is hateful about war. If we are to vote about getting into war, why don't they limit the voters to men between twenty-one and forty-five who have to fight.

Perhaps, mother-love is the biggest farce on earth. If it were real we wouldn't have any wars. If most of us took our religion sincerely, as a real thing, of course we would have no war. Now they tear up copies of *All Quiet On The Western Front* to throw down on Broadway in welcome to someone who invents a new machine of war.

God must be awfully far away or disinterested to let people go on living the way they do in dirt and in filthy holes contaminating one another, swarming out to kill when ordered.

They say that love makes the world go round. More likely, in our social set-up, it is the inferiority complex. It makes people want to get ahead, be important. The spirit of competition must be kept out of the artist's mind.

I have never been interested in painting or doing things that I know I can paint or do. I get an attack of enthusiasm once in a while that lasts me for several years. It is both good and bad for my work. When I have carried some pictures through to a fairly successful conclusion, I want to go on and paint something different. On the other hand, maybe I don't stick to one kind of thing long enough.

CHAPTER II

POINT OF VIEW ABOUT TEACHING

IF I AM USEFUL as a teacher it is because I have dug into my own work. Teaching lashes me into a state of consciousness; I find myself trying to prove in my work some of the things I dig out of my sub-conscious to pass on to others. Many an instructor passes on only what he learned as a student. But an artist today, if he has assimilated the meaning of the ultra-modern movement, may have advanced to a greater understanding of the meaning of art than he had thirty years ago. In the last hundred years art has been so diseased by the influence of the camera that any creative artist who is conscious of the technique of tradition should endeavor to pass on what he can about the language of art.

In my student days there was a great deal of emphasis on inspiration, self-expression, wit, and pictorial beauty. Robert Henri was the great teacher of this school. Because he was an American creative artist he was a preacher. He was also a great painter. He had the ability to arouse the creative spirit in almost anyone. When he took hold of an able and interested student he could bring out all the latent talent. It was through the weekly "open house" sessions in his studio that many who are now well-known were encouraged to become painters.

Henri gave much of his time to seeing students and writing letters to artists who sent him work from all parts of the country. His interest in art movements that have opened up opportunities for young artists, can never be adequately appreciated. His fight against the dominance of the National Academy, his fight for the

Independent Artists, and the MacDowell groups, his influence on the Art Students League to keep progressive teachers on the staff —all these and many other fights did a great deal for the healthy condition of American art today. I have tried to go on from the inspirational teaching of Henri to give my students more technical information about how to think and do.

Remarks To New Students:

Again and again, I have said: I don't want to interfere with your way of seeing, if you are seeing Things. I have no tricks to teach you. I don't want to teach you any one way to draw. I don't want to teach you my opinions, but if you can get hold of my point of view I don't think it will hurt you. I am here to help you. I want to help you find a purpose, a reason for painting. I can tell you some things about the "how" to paint. Not any one "how". Then you must find your way through your own experience and hard work.

I can't teach you how to become commercial successes. I can't teach you to be illustrators, or how to make money doing advertising work. All the men who are getting there in advertising set out to be real artists.

People who take things too literally don't get much of anything from my teaching. By never saying anything I mean, I say a great deal. I never mean anything I say under oath. I never mean exactly what I say. Not even this. You have to read between the words.

Teaching has taken years of my life. But I feel that I must do it, that I must reach as many students as I can to arouse in them the creative spirit, and to teach them as best I can, some of the technique of the great tradition of art.

Bernard Shaw once said, "He who can, does. He who cannot, teaches." And some cannot teach. Now you may ask why am I here? Because I am a failure as a rent-payer, not as a painter.

[7]

I'm not just a nice old man coming to see you young folks twice a week. I'm not flirting, playing around. I'm serious about it. I am giving years of my life to do this. But we are here to play, to play because we are serious about it. Here we are, put on the most insignificant speck of dust in the universe, left for a while with a lot of other worms. If you don't want to be serious about playing, do something of no account. Go into banking. Buy collar buttons at five cents a dozen and sell them for five cents a piece.

This class is a laboratory where you can work out ideas and have me around to give you the benefit of my experience. If you can't stand a scolding that is given with the earnest desire of helping you, you don't belong here. Go into some class where you won't learn anything, where the instructor pats you on the back and quotes poetry.

We are all students and we always will be. Learn to yearn. Never spare yourself from hard work and the yearning to understand. Search into the meaning of things, the reality of life. We are just paving the way for some genius who will come along and consummate our efforts. Teaching makes me tired and often cross, but I am trying to pass on to you some of the things I have discovered. Fortunately, few are new.

It takes a great deal of strong personality to survive the art school training. Hard nuts that the art schools can't crack and devour get through and become artists.

No one living has the authority to say that the personal expression of any one of his contemporaries is absolutely bad.

Why is it that so many people who get old get dyspeptic or get wise? I am just on the verge, and will certainly get one or the other.

A negative, anti-thing can't be great. Anti-bad art, anti-liquor, for instance. I am anti-prohibition, but two negatives equal an affirmative. I am not anti-saloon. The kind of art made for any anti-reason, anti-war, anti-humanity, and so forth, can't be great art. It can be important propaganda, satire, but not great art.

No great poet, no great artist ever allows facts to interfere with the truth. Facts are not necessarily truth. Poetry can convey the truth more than a statement of fact. The history of the Civil War has more meaning through the book, *John Brown's Body*, than it has through the facts of history.

Most plays are sums of facts. I rather think a play should be made up of untruths, to bring out some of the deep truth of life. Shakespeare did not hesitate to distort facts to expose truths about human nature. All of his work has a quality of punning, only he did it with ideas as well as word sounds.

Art comes from leisure and not from industry. I believe Plato said that.

Work for yourself first. You can paint best the things you like or the things you hate. You cannot paint well when indifferent. Express a mental opinion about something you are sensitive to in life around you. There is a profound difference between sentimentality and sensitivity. Artists are sensitive to life. If you start out with sentimentality where will you end?

Anyone who has something to say will find someone who is interested in his work. What difference does it make whether your work is appreciated or not? The work will still be yours. Anyway, most of us are only appreciated after we are dead.

Painting must have some stimulus. Keep the mainspring of life which gives you the creative urge. Keep your humanity.

When you have found something about people or nature that you want to talk about graphically, you will find a technical way to say those things. Find something that you care about saying, even if it has been said before.

The Teacher's Responsibility

Several years ago a New York newspaper designated me in a series of articles, "Town Types," as "one of the old familiar ones."

[9]

I was sub-titled, "an unbearded Tolstoi, a lot more sensible æsthetically." Maybe Douglas Gilbert was right about me. At any rate he wrote an amusing interview, and it is always a relief not to be too much mis-quoted, especially if one has definite ideas about art—anybody's art. I won't try to define it now; most students with whom I have come in contact and who are doing interesting work do not go in for specific definitions of anything. They are always looking, but never entirely satisfied.

That is the reason that helping students of art has always interested me, and the reason that my efforts as a teacher at the Art Students League for the last twenty-four years,—although having certain drawbacks as far as the time element and its effect on my own work are concerned,—have nevertheless maintained an attraction for me. Teaching has been, in spite of the extra exertion, a valuable stimulant to my own work.

It is for these reasons that I believe that a message I wrote to the Art Students League on assuming the Presidency of the Board of Control may have some permanent interest.

"Although for sixteen years I had been an instructor at the Art Students League and as such familiar with the scope of its functions and its daily routine, upon my election as President of the League I became impressed with the importance of my position.

I believe the League to be the largest and most successful cooperative art institution in this country. Without endowment, purely under the administration of its own artists and students, it is financially sound, and a demonstration of the fact that the artist is not, as so often rated, an inferior business man.

Maybe it is because I am new on the job, or maybe it is because I was put under a $50,000 bond which the League Constitution requires of the head of the Board of Control, I repeat, I am impressed, and I feel a great sense of responsibility. I thought I had taught long enough to have a pretty good idea of what it was all about. Now I think it might be a good idea to have some of the teachers bonded too. Not because of any financial irresponsibility—oh, no! But maybe just to make them feel their responsibility in teaching art. I confess I had much less consciousness of responsibility as a teacher than I have as President.

One reason why the League is first among the art schools of this country is the fact that it furnishes such a varied menu of nourishment for a hungry art student, ranging from the conservative to the most ultra-modern. A student at the League can choose his art studies much as he can choose food at an automat. He may shop around and even provide himself with materials for indigestion. But it is this very feature that is one of the most important in his progress, providing he keeps his mind open. Too many students at the League have settled down to be fighting advocates of some particular one or the other of the delicacies to be found in the League's bill of fare. So, we have people frothing at the mouth and fighting for the preëminence of pie, while others are devoted to the interests of soup. Some are, figuratively speaking, rabid vegetarians and still others stick to a strict meat diet.

Of course, this is a little like a political speech from a perambulator, but it does reflect life and it is probably invaluable in a school which provides so much opportunity for so many varying points of view.

A student at the League should therefore cultivate an attitude toward his studies which is both flexible and critical. It should be flexible enough so that he can change his mind as often as need be; and it should be critical in that he need not take either the professed 'modern' or the professed 'conservative' at their own evaluation.

Good modern artists are the conservative artists who follow the fine old tradition of setting down a concept in painting. They jump over the period of the past seventy-five years of degeneration due perhaps to the influence of the camera which gives a reflected visual image. This visual painting is still being done today by

[11]

the so-called 'conservative' academicians who have no tradition behind them other than the camera.

Many intelligent people have accepted the false idea that accuracy in representing visual facts is a sign of progress in art. Such imitation of superficial effects has nothing to do with art, which is and always has been the making of mental concepts. Even the scientist is interested in effects only as phenomena from which to deduce order in life.

The good ultra-modern artist as a teacher puts his students through a thorough, hard, and rigorous training apart from the visual aspect of things, teaching them to put their mental processes into their painting. That is why work away from the model is often better than with the model before one. In the presence of the model, the student is tempted to look and reproduce something that 'looks like' the model, while it would be better for him to put down his mental image of the model from memory. I might add, incidentally, and as a 'terrible example', that all of my early paintings, including my old city street life paintings, were done from memory.

'Looks like' is not the test of a good painting. It indicates merely visual similarity and shows that the artist has not put his brain to work. If, before transmitting to canvas what the eye casually beholds, the artist will spend some time in the study of his subject matter, the result rendered will more likely be a solid concept and not a mere general aspect.

Every art student should paint the simple solids: that is, spheres, cubes, cylinders, pyramids, and cones. Everyone knows these forms mentally. Therein lies their importance. Still lifes as set up in most art classes are too complicated. The eye of the student is diverted from the simple basic forms which they actually conceal, and he tries to get his painting to 'look like the things look', thereby falling into the error of the casual aspect.

In an article in the March, 1931 number of *The Arts*, we are told that Thomas Eakins always insisted on his students painting simple studies of such things as an egg, a lump of sugar, or a piece of chalk to try to get the texture. Texture is one of the great pitfalls. Many artists have had reputations built up on their so-called mastery of texture, notably Sargent. But Sargent did not know how to paint texture. Yes, he could paint satin, but then everything he painted he made satin. The texture of realization is what counts, not realism.

A still life which I would set up would consist of a white tablecloth, an egg, and an ordinary yellow earthenware plate.

If I had my way, I would equip an art school with hundreds, no, thousands, of the simple solids, in different sizes, covered with all sorts of materials including cloths of all textures and surfaces, metals of all hues, woods of all kinds, rough, smooth, polished. And the student would draw and paint these for a couple of years with figure drawing on the side for dessert.

Even with his dessert, however, the artist should learn to find these basic forms. Cézanne said that the five simple solids are all there is to nature. It is the ability to feel this when painting a human face, for instance, that makes for artistic understanding. To bring this about, the student should learn to imagine a cylinder which has a hemispherical top for the head; put a half cone before it for a nose, then take two reversed hollow spheres for the eyes with solid spheres set in them for eyeballs. The mouth is a truncated cone which does not begin directly underneath the nose but extends all the way back to the ears following the line of the jaws. In this way he will learn constantly to analyze apparently complicated structures into the simple basic forms. How clearly some modernist experiments have shown this!

There, you see I slip back into teaching at the slightest chance —which proves that I'm not yet really inured to the office of the President of the Board of Control."

When a person reaches my age (three-score and some) if he

is an artist he is aware of life. He has learned to keep in touch with his generation, and every generation is *The* generation to an artist. But none of us lives in an unchanging world. We have to meet the world we are in as it comes along. Many people think of an artist as a recluse. I think that *an artist is a spectator* who not only sees, but interprets. He has to be alone to interpret but he has to be abroad to see.

To be a spectator one does not need to have experiences. The artist does not need to touch the thing he is working from. His imagination and understanding are based upon his ability to project himself into the outside world. He possesses ideas, images, in his mind. Maybe the mountains and deserts are a part of him. I have enjoyed them, painted them. In that sense they belong to me. Likewise, the person who owns a picture is not its consumer unless he appreciates it.

Perhaps it is the evidence of seeing and remembering that has interested me so much in the work of the unrecognized American Indian artists.

The work of students of art makes me feel like giving them from my store of life and art. When I think they see and remember and that some may be able to interpret in color, design, plaster, or what they please, I feel a definite interest in how they do it. If the Society of Independent Artists, for instance, only introduced to the small, appreciative audience of art lovers, one artist of significance a year, I would think that show worth while. That it has produced more is gratifying. And I, for one, can never be disinterested in the person who attempts to use the language of the brush, the chisel, the etching needle, or the crayon.

I am not advising anyone, old or young, to become an artist, but I will say that it is a highly satisfying life. That fact you, yourself, must know, just as you know that it seems completely discouraging at times.

How far a person can go with his art depends on what is within himself to go on. This qualification is not inherited, for it means about one hundred per cent hard work plus an interest in what is going on around you and a conception of your own which comes, not from copying, but from producing or creating.

Artists are not bound by positive limitation. They see. They know what to eliminate as well as what to include. They know (and knowledge does not come from a limited experience) just how to interpret their outlook on life.

I have never been outside the United States, but while this fact means that I have seen few of the masterpieces of the past, it may mean that I have got my own share here and now. Perhaps I agree with the Chinese philosopher who said that if you stayed in one spot, all the world would come to you.

My Contribution

Back in the Nineties our gods were Whistler, Velasquez, and Frans Hals. We were too much concerned with getting the impression of the moment, the beauty of easy brushwork, the surfaces of things. But because I made my living as an illustrator, my drawings were all done from memory and so were most of my early paintings. No one can remember the visual appearance of a thing, but memory can recall the Thing itself. For this reason my early work is not without artistic merit. All fine art is the result of the artist coming to grips with the reality of things. Also because I was a draughtsman using the pen and etching needle, I was using these tools to make things with signs. Every line is a sign unless used to imitate appearances.

When the work of the ultra-modern artists was brought to this country by Alfred Stieglitz and the Armory Show, I consciously began to be aware of the technique of art: the use of graphic devices to represent plastic forms. While I have made no abstract pictures, I have absorbed a great deal from the work of the ultra-moderns. Through a study of the moderns and the working out of plastic problems in my own painting, I have arrived at a greater valuation of the old masters than I had thirty years ago. I wish I had known then what I know now and had thirty years more to live.

My greatest interest is in the European tradition of three-dimensional painting, particularly the painting of life around me. While my work is sufficient evidence that the city streets and landscape have afforded me a rich subject matter, there is now a prevailing idea that I am no longer painting "Sloans" because I am also doing figures and portraits. These subjects are just as much part of my life experience as the teeming streets of New York. To have the subject in front of you while you work, makes the artistic problem much greater. For to paint from what is in front of you as though you were painting from memory, using the model as an inspiration for an exciting plastic design, requires more *mental technique* than to paint from memory alone.

No apology need be made for what is commonly misnamed an "easel painter." The small picture which is painted for the artist himself has a special integrity of expression and fire of its own which a mural that is made for the public consumption cannot have. A mural is like a speech or epic, but there is also room for the lyric poem or essay. The small picture in the hands of a master like Rembrandt, is one of the highest forms of human expression. It is a precious thing like a gem, in which the artist can concentrate the full powers of his ability and understanding.

I have only a few things to say to the student, but it is necessary to say them over in many ways to make the points clear. They are mostly technical: The importance of the mental technique of seeing things; an emphasis on plastic consciousness; the fact that all things in nature are composed of variations of the five simple solids: cube, cone, sphere, cylinder, and pyramid; the significance of devices in drawing, by which we represent three-dimensional forms on a two-dimensional surface; the low relief concept of composition; the importance of foreshortening rather than visual perspective in signifying spacial projection and recession; the use of color as a graphic tool; emphasis on realization rather than realism as the essential character of reality in art.

I think my own real contribution is the analysis of the separation of form and color as an aesthetic quality. The separation of form and color through the technical process of underpainting and glazing gives realization that cannot be achieved in direct painting; although direct painting may bring splendid results with the principle in mind: witness Van Gogh. Whenever Van Gogh drew a line on top of the color surface he was separating form and color. I believe the artist should be conscious of the separation while drawing: think of the form first, and then the color texture.

CHAPTER III

POINT OF VIEW ABOUT ART

ART SPRINGS FROM AN INTEREST IN LIFE but it isn't art if it ends there. The *art life* of a thing created by man comes through the use of symbols combined to make images of ideas. These images, when projected in form understandable to the senses of other human beings, are works of art, artifices. The prehistoric man drawing with a blunt tool on the wall of a cave made an image of an animal —he made art. Every word is an image, a symbol. The writer automatically uses symbols. The word *animal* does not look like the thing but is a symbol for the communication of the idea.

Drawing is one of the three means of communication between spirits, like speech and music. You wouldn't say nowadays, with pride, "I can't understand a book. I never learned how to read." Everybody should be able to draw a little the way we write a little or whistle. One reason for the existence of art students and artists is the desire to acquire an additional means of self-expression. In school we may learn our craft but we learn to become artists by making contacts with the world. There must be a desire to express the inner life we have felt and lived.

Art is an ideograph. So long as you are not making ideas you are not making art. The artist forms concepts of what he has observed in nature. He crystallizes the prose of nature into poetic images. Art is the result of the creative urge of life consciousness. It is the graphics of ideas.

The artist has an ability to see nature and form his own concept. Beyond that he must have some creative imagination, that faculty for materializing his vision of nature in the medium he has chosen.

There is such a thing as looking at nature too calmly, without any excitement. The artist must get a kick out of something in nature before he can create. If you only get a kick out of other works of art you should not be an artist. You should be a connoisseur, or a buyer or a consumer of art.

A critic once asked Degas, "What is this thing, art? What is it all about?" And Degas said, "Well, I have spent my life trying to find out and if I had found out I would have done something about it long ago." He did not specify what. But he could not have done more than he did do in painting his pictures.

You may define art, but you cannot define good art. Art is not like grammar; there is no good grammar and bad grammar. There is good and bad art.

Good art cannot be defined because such a definition would have to include the word *beauty*. People have written volumes to define the word beauty, and I can't believe that the books would have been so long if they had found the definition. My own definition of art does not specify good art: *Art is the result of a creative impulse derived out of a consciousness of life.*

If the work looks as though the artist made it to look like something else that sold for a thousand dollars, if that was the motive behind the work, it is not art because it didn't come from life consciousness and a creative impulse.

An imitative impulse is to repeat something, while a creative impulse is to make something with mental control brought to bear on the material which the eye brings to the mind. The mind adds its consciousness of, and experience with reality to anything that is seen by the eye. The reason an engineer knows the tracks ahead of him are the same distance apart is because they seem to be coming together. His mental experience with this visual phenomenon tells him the tracks are parallel.

The artist has this consciousness of reality in life around him, and also in the life within him which is just as real. Possibly it is more real than the life around him because it is the life within him applied to the life without, which really gives him his creative consciousness. Many people either never have it or else it is atrophied.

An artist gets in contact with real things. He establishes contact in a way others do not. He is in contact with animate and inanimate nature. He sees the desert and feels the great creative spirit of natural forces. He can project himself into nature about him. He can look at a cat on the back fence and feel as that cat feels and, in a sense, know what that cat thinks. The artist does not need to experience to understand. While he is the custodian of life consciousness, nevertheless, he remains a spectator. He maintains a spectator's attitude toward life.

He seeks to find order in life, and to invent ways to put that sense of order in his work as a document of his understanding. Even a half-way good picture has had more of this establishment of order in the making of it than the layman is ever conscious of. The artist's business is the placing of things in order; his mind takes creative impulses from life and places them on canvas, arranges them in the words of poetry or the notes of music, so others can follow and find what he sought for them.

A work of art, a creative impulse, does not have to spring from liking, from love, from an admiration of the subject. In fact one quality of "would-be" art is that it does spring too much from a cheap kind of liking. Art generally comes from liking things but it can also be the child of hate or dislike. Hogarth's work is a good example of that. Many of his pictures were a sort of tirade, diatribe on the manners and ways he disliked. And yet, if you like the kind of life he is portraying in his sermon pictures, you will find that he hasn't spoiled it for you. Take that series of the *Rake's Progress*. He takes you behind the scenes with players in their dressing rooms, smelly dirty places, but such jolly places to be—he gets that over in spite of the fact that it was hatred of that sort of life which led him to draw it.

The artist has to find something in or about life which interests him. He has to pause and select the elements that will put his idea across. It doesn't have to be some great tragic event; just a couple of plums on a plate, seen with the mind, will suffice for subject matter. A man like Renoir puts three plums on a plate and turns the surface of an eight by twelve inch canvas into a result that is as æsthetically vivid as a piece of carved relief.

The real tools of the artist are graphic signs made of line, tone, and color, combined to make images of things. A child's drawing of a hand made of a square with four lines sticking out for fingers and another for a thumb, is a sign or image for a hand. Every word is an image-symbol. The real vitality in a work of art comes through the use of sign inventions, devices to convey plastic ideas.

One of my ideas about technique is that I regard the mind itself as a tool. Most artists paint as though they had no minds. Their paintings look as though they were made from eye to hand with no intervention by the brain. That isn't art. Art is the response of the living to life. It is therefore the record left behind by civilization.

I believe that my definition of art includes the art craftsman,— the true artisan—the man who feels the need to express some creative appreciation for life even when making a chair or weaving a rug. The craftsmen are being squeezed out of existence by machines. A man who shoves a bolt into a passing car and then shoves a bolt into another passing car, and so on, can't be expected to have much pride when he sees a Ford roll by. He can't have the pride that an artist workman has who has made something himself.

The work of the American Indians is a perfect demonstration that things not generally regarded as works of graphic or plastic art, are indeed the works of artists. Their pots, blankets, paintings are so evidently inspired by a consciousness of life, plus a thing we have not got—a great tradition.

It might be said that there is no real traditional art in the world today except in the work of the Indians. None of the great nations are really following traditions in the sense that the Gothic period had tradition. The Indians have a great traditional base. They work together with the same feeling of being a part of the community that inspired the unknown artists of the great Gothic period. Certain conditions in the social relations of men must change before we will have any return of that kind of united spirit, which, running through the artists, will make them work together.

We have only a carry-over of the European tradition as it has been maintained by the French. The French school is the only one that has survived in a healthy way during the past two hundred years. With regard to the other schools we are always speaking of the art of the past. Is there any Dutch art, English art, German art, Spanish art or even Japanese art today? Certainly there is no Italian art today, but there is the great Italian cultural heritage from past centuries. Art has stopped, if not died, in most of the countries where it flourished of old.

The tradition we have inherited from France is one of individualism. I think art would be greater if we could lose some of that intense individualism. When it is less evident, the most impressive work is made, gigantic efforts of the human mind and hand—truly social documents, with no name to be found on them anywhere. Today we paint a picture and cannot wait to put our little name in the corner. That is all right, but it might be better if the work were anonymous.

I believe there is no progress in art. While we may derive our impulses from different subject matter than the artist of four hundred years ago, the underlying purpose is just the same. The man who scratched his concepts of animals on the roof of a cave in Spain thousands of years ago, just had a space to work on and something to work with and he put down his ideas. That is what the artist does today. I never could agree with the ultra-modern artists who wanted to burn the paintings in the museums, implying that what they were doing was progress. There isn't any advance. Some art is greater than other art, but there is no change in the inherent character of art. The mental technique today is the same as it was fifty thousand years ago.

One phase that was mistaken for progress in art was the clever eyesight painting that came in with the influence of the camera. Maybe the degeneration of art started with the discovery of scientific perspective. Any standard of art based on visual verisimilitude has nothing to do with the root principle of art. Art springs from an interest in reality, the concept of the thing itself.

Aesthetic Consumers

The artist paints first of all for himself, but the very next person he paints for is the æsthetic consumer, the person who is equipped to enjoy and appreciate. His point of view very often is broader than the creative artist's. He may have a taste for a number of kinds of art. There are some artists who are too much appreciators and enjoyers of the finished product of others to be able to create themselves. It brings about a kind of inferiority complex that prevents the creative spirit from functioning. Suppose I knew all the art in the world, I would think, what is the use of my painting. I might have an idea, a concept that wanted to come out, but with all this consciousness of and admiration for the glorious things that the creative minds of the world had already produced, what would be the use of my trying to do anything. I'll stack saucers in the nearest cafe. That attitude has stopped many a sensitive artist at the beginning of his career.

The æsthetic consumer is a person who gives some time to pictures, studies them, gets acquainted with them. Pictures are like people, you get to know them through long acquaintance. The consumer is glad to meet new pictures; he likes and dislikes according to his own judgment.

You don't have to understand pictures. I really feel that an artist can make a good one without understanding it. Most people think that they understand a picture when they have recognized the subject. That isn't understanding. I like the slang expression "to get" the picture. You can say that about any kind of work, representational or abstract, if you pay enough attention to it. You can't expect to know a picture at a casual glance. It may be that when you really know them, you will learn to like the ones you disliked at first.

A man who owns a work of art is not necessarily an æsthetic consumer. A consumer may be an owner but a consumer is not necessarily an owner. The owner has no right to destroy a work of art; he can consume it by appreciation but in no other way. A consumer of art is different from a consumer of a boiled egg: one can consume a work of art and still have it.

The buying of art comes from so tremendously different motives. Few buyers buy because they like the work themselves. First of all, the buying of well known pictures at high prices has been very logically proved to be one of the conspicuous wastes. The buying of any picture is a waste of money from the American point of view, and the buying of a very high priced picture is a conspicuous waste that will be heralded in the newspapers. People buy pictures to prove that they have money. The gods of the business man are money and power. Money brings no power except over cowards. There is only one kind of power worth having and that is power over one's self. Many people think that will power is something worth while. John Butler Yeats, painter, father of the Irish poet, said, "Will power is the poorest equipment that an artist can have. No artist could have it and be a really effective artist. If Shakespeare had had will power he could never have written his plays."

Another usual reason for buying pictures is that it leads to a kind of social success. There is no quicker way to find your name in the papers regularly than by starting a collection of pictures. Another thing, if you buy several pictures, you can write books on art. It makes you feel that you are an authority, have culture.

Some people buy art as an investment. The man who owns an undisputed Rembrandt has something with more value than any other thing in his possession. Of this world's holdings, a vital work of art is an investment more secure than anything else, save perhaps gold bullion.

The real collector of art buys what he likes, lives with the pictures, discards some, and buys again. The price of a picture is no indication of its worth. Good pictures, good contemporary pictures don't cost much. The best artists who are painting for themselves don't expect to make a living at painting, and price their work within the reach of the average person. You can buy a topnotch painting for the price of a cheap second-hand car, or a fine print for the price of a couple of theatre tickets.

Take the case of Albert C. Barnes, the most important modern collector in America. When he started he had the ordinary rich man's collection and had spent many thousands of dollars. He told Glackens that he had acquired paintings from the best dealers in New York and Philadelphia. Glackens said, "I know what you have. A couple of Millets, red heads by Henner, a Diaz, and fuzzy Corots. They are just stinging you as they do everybody who has money to spend." Barnes was a practical man and didn't like that idea. But Glackens told him to put those things in his attic and it was arranged that Glackens should take a letter of credit and go to Paris. There he bought the nucleus of the A. C. Barnes collection of modern pictures: Renoirs, Cézannes, Matisses, and many others but particularly he laid stress on the Renoirs. That started Barnes on the right track. He began to live with those pictures, studied them, and bought more of them. He weeded out the old ones and sold off those he no longer cared for. Today he knows more about Art than any artist needs to know.

Like, buy, learn better, sell, and buy again. Just buy what you like. Most people are afraid to do that because somebody will come along who they think knows more about art than they do. Among the pictures you dislike today are the ones you will like later, if your taste improves. This is true of Dr. Bode, Thomas Craven, or anyone. If you have any other point of view there is too much conceit in your personal opinion.

They say that art is a luxury because of the depression. But I really believe that this is the time when people should turn to the artists. Not the artists whose work is selling for thousands, but the interesting work of men who sell their things at reasonable figures. I believe the work of artists, poets, musicians, is a kind of food for starving souls, as necessary as food for the body. Why should we worry about feeding bodies if they have starving souls? Unless it is a case of fuel and oil to keep a dumb machine working that can work only so many hours without them. Wherever there is intelligence and the soul is starving, there is no use worrying whether the body starves or not. That may sound churchy but I don't mean it so. Select your own soul-food in the way of art. If indigestion sets in you need a change, and you can find a food that digests better.

You Can't Make a Living at Art

The idea of taking up art as a calling, a trade, a profession, is a mirage. Art enriches life. It makes life worth living. But to make a living at it—that idea is incompatible with making art.

This idea of making a living at art first occurs to parents. The plain fact is that it can't be done. As a matter of fact you can't "on your own" make a living at plumbing or any other kind of honest labor. You can't make a living at anything without doing your share to make a thousand times better living for someone else.

The phrase "making a living" implies only existence, anyhow.

Then there is this idea that the world owes you a living. Here is a little thought about that. It isn't particularly logical but it makes my point. You were paid when you were born, with the privilege of living. Death is all that is coming to you. Life came to you when you were born.

Shun this idea of going into art with success as an aim, wealth as an aim, for the purpose of getting on in the world, getting the good things in life. Success has apparently become much more the art student's aim than it was in my time. It spells disaster. No one who sets out for success gets the real thing. All you can get is a little sauce poured over you while you are alive. You may achieve a car, a good car to bump into other cars less good or better.

Success, what do we mean by it? Sargent was supposed to be a success. He painted his picture, an expensive conglomeration of oil paint marks imitating the light and shadow shapes on faces, furniture, and satin dresses—he painted that picture over and over again. He was decorated and lionized, made a lot of money. And what is his status today? How long did that kind of success last? There is only one thing to do about success—shun it. The only kind of success to desire is success with yourself. To make steps, progress, with yourself.

Today the artist is constantly questioning himself, "What am I doing, is it art?" That is a very irrelevant question. The real creative artist doesn't care whether his work is art or not. He has his work to do, is driven by a creative fire. He can't concern himself with whether what he is doing is art.

Who is to answer the question, what is art? Today there are lots of opportunities for the young artist who is beginning to produce, lots of sources from which to find out what is art. There is the government. You can get assistance from the government in deciding. For ten years I advocated off and on, mostly off, that the government take an interest in art. Many people are now asking the government to do so, people who opposed me years ago when I was urging governmental interest in art.

I want a Department of Art in the government because I think it would dignify the profession. The government spends money on utilities, why should it not spend money on the spiritual utilities, the things which are the really civilizing instruments of humanity. France has had a department of art for over a hundred years, and France is the most art conscious country in the world. The art selected by the government isn't always the best. But the fact that the government takes an interest and supports art financially, raises the level of the profession, increases public interest.

Of course, alas, as the government takes up art, it will gradually establish standards, standards of mediocrity, because any matter of taste which is decided by vote is bound to be influenced by the bad taste of the majority. But I want to see these standards set up by an organization that is really national, not one like the National Academy which is a private institution and no more a National agency than the National Biscuit Company.

When these governmental agencies, commissions, get to work deciding about art they remind me of a cattle ranch. Did you ever see a round up and branding? Well, these government authorities on art are the punchers, the cattle branders. I suppose we can all hope that if our work is found good by the government, we will feel the brand on our left hip.

I have other reasons sincere enough, for wanting to see the government in art. I am Irish, and so I am naturally "agin the government." In government can lurk the foes of all that is best in human life. I want to be able to differ with the government all along the line. I hate nearly everything else it does, its support of privilege, the wars it gets us into. Why shouldn't I hate it in my own line, my own calling. Having the government the advocate of the mediocre in art, the employer of art, would be a good thing.

We would know where to locate the enemy. Until we have a Department of Art I shall have to vent my scorn on the National Academy. I have been flattering them thus for twenty-five years. I want to have something higher up, more worthwhile, to villify.

Don't think I am not in favor of having the government support the arts. The art projects set up during the depression have done more to stimulate art in America than any other movement in the past three hundred years. But in the light of history you can be sure that any organization set up to promote culture will become an institution and carry on only second-rate ideas. The stronger the institution the less chance there is of its retaining vigor through changes within itself. A few people get hold of the paying jobs and they rule the roost. Wherever you have economics mixed up with art, there you have politics.

When you get to the point where you begin to step into organizations and put letters after your name, you begin to look down on others from the gutter. And I wonder how you can look down from the gutter! One can imagine a bum lying in the gutter, with a mirror in his hand. He lays his mirror in the mud, looks into it, and says, "Thank God, there is somebody below me!"

Our conservative academies don't carry on the tradition of painting Things. They have degenerated into superficial training of the eye and hand for eyesight painting that has nothing to do with art. They give prizes for the best of these facile or clumsy imitations of the appearance of nature. The better the imitation the larger the award. They implant the virus of competition.

When you enter one of these institutions you get a musty whiff, that old cathedral smell. Here are the habitual art students, wishfully yearning to draw, and being praised twice a week. They make tedious charcoal drawings. A charcoal paper with a bromidic smudge on it results from a week's work with stump and chamois. The people who made those drawings were once innocent human beings, people with a desire to be artists. Now they are like the blind led by the blind. This sort of teaching is a septic influence. Walter Pach's *Ananias: or The False Artist* did a great deal to expose the institutions and artists who betray their noble calling. Since we have to speak well of the dead let us knock them while they are still alive.

The jury system is a cherisher of the commonplace. The only kind of jury that is of any use gives proportional representation to each brand of art represented by a member of the committee. If there is one progressive member to three conservative members he should have a right to select one-fourth of the pictures in the exhibition. Otherwise, the other three votes control the entire selection of pictures. It is just a joke when they put a progressive name or two on most juries.

Voting in matters of taste can never result in the selection of the best work. All the greatest artists were not recognized by the majority of their contemporaries, either artists or critics.

The juries and exhibitions today are going in for stylized work, the American Scene. Good pictures which are concerned with less static, spectacular realism, do not pass the juries because their style is not in fashion today. Juries and museums recognize what is in fashion; they are fashion experts. The mode today is a kind of sentimental realism, related to the Rogers groups of the last century.

There is another place to turn to when you want to find out if your art is good. The critics. They are paid for telling artists whether their art is good or not. They can extol; they can condemn. There are two places of honor, the extolled and the condemned: You will think success is knocking at the door. And they can ignore. That is the worst they can do to you. (But you can get into the paper some other way—a little racketeering or second-story work.) I suppose I should know. I have even been accused of being a publicity hound. I think it is because I have a quick and bitter tongue. When a reporter calls me up to get some ideas about what has happened I often have some sourish things to say. There are other reasons. Anyone who has been in the newspaper business as long as I, may get special attention in the press. Certainly no one can accuse me of selling my work through publicity. I have had lots of it and never sold a painting until I was forty-nine years old, and not very many since. No, I have some ability to get art matters into the news through my sharp but honest tongue, and I have used that to further the cause of many art movements from the Society of Independent Artists to the work of the American Indian.

The dealers, too, will tell you if your work is worthwhile, if they look at your work at all. They have a pretty well fortified position. The artist's relation with the dealer might be explained thus: You make confectionery, say chewing gum, and the dealer proposes that, if your gum is a new and little known brand he might take it on a sixty-forty basis. You get forty percent and the dealer gets sixty percent. But if it is an old, more-used gum, he would take forty and you sixty. He says, "I'll take your gum and I'll provide the show case. If any is sold I'll give you part of the money. If it becomes popular I may increase your share." So that is another place to find out.

There is one other place to find out if what you are doing is art—within your own honest judgment. Art is something which has been created in response to an urge that came through contact with life. The critics, the dealers, the government—are trying to define good art. There never will be any standard of art. What a terrible thing it would be if everyone knew and agreed upon what was good. A definition defines, puts up markers, says that something can be analyzed into black and white. Anything is art that originated as a response to life. That is a pretty broad category, but it gives you a yardstick that rules out a lot of things.

I am making no plea for conservative art. There are other things that are nothing but technical drill which, because of their relationship to art that is made in response to life, must be included as worthwhile. I am keenly alive to the importance of ultra-modern art, which is valuable in the study of technique. I believe in five or even ten years of enthusiastic technical study. Study of the old masters through Picasso and Braque, Cézanne and Renoir. I regard all but a handful of the moderns as disseminators of technique. Young people are always throwing themselves into one camp or another, conservative or progressive. I regard the conservative camp of today, the academic work made today as a visual imitative effort that has nothing at all to do with art.

That I am alive, it hurts me to confess, does not prove that one can make a living at art. The fact that men decorated with parts of the word *Ananias* make a living selling canvas with oil paint on it doesn't prove that you can make a living at art. That which you make for yourself, that you make for nobody else—you won't make a living from that. I have made a living. I have been able to scratch enough together to pay the rent from the time when it was twelve dollars a month including gas, to a time, not so far away, when it was two hundred and fifty a month. I didn't make a living from the pictures I made for myself, but by illustrating and teaching.

If making pictures that somebody buys makes the art commercial,—Picasso is a commercial artist. So was Van Gogh, but not while he was alive. Why does Van Gogh get on the front page of the paper? Because he is a great artist? No. It is the sob story about his life that gets him on the first page. Now the critics recognize him, are proud of it. Do our critics think they are superior to the French critics of the 1870's who condemned Van Gogh? Art criticism in this country is in its infancy. France has had it for three hundred years. I am no good at dates—I may have understated it by a thousand years. You can be quite sure that any art critic we have today is missing the Van Gogh of today, just as the French critics did in the Nineteenth Century. Van

Gogh received a hundred and nine dollars for his work while he was alive and now some of his pictures sell for fifty thousand dollars. Was Van Gogh a success? From the commonplace point of view he was not. But I think he was a success. Reading through his letters, you will find that he felt he was a success with himself. But not with the academy, the juries, the dealers. His art was the product of his inner self in response to the life around him.

If you are a success in your lifetime you are almost sure to be forgotten afterwards, almost without exception. One such was Rubens; he was a success. But he did something most artists don't like to do. He learned his trade and practised it like a bricklayer. He was practically the same artist when he was twenty-five as when he died. He wrote those pictures like a man writing visiting cards at a county fair. The technique of Rubens was a mighty technique, something that seems to have left us in the last hundred years. He was a great artist, great in his own lifetime. There may be other examples of the exception to the rule.

I have tried to function as an artist, doing the things I wanted to do; sometimes because somebody wanted me to do something else. An artist can be independent as an artist. He can't be independent as a human individual. Times were better for the artist when, to make a living, you could get a job washing dishes at night. This kind of artists' jobs is gone. There are five hundred people waiting for one job now.

We artists who paint for ourselves are not in the same boat with carpenters and bricklayers who rightly demand work. We can't point back to the time when we made a living at art. I am all for the working people organizing to protect themselves. For many years I was an active Socialist and even ran for office! But I draw a distinction between an artist and a working-man, a craftsman. The artist, the real artist, must work for himself. Artists who classify themselves as tradesmen have given up their birthright to independent thought. There is only one creative action in the world

[33]

today that has any right to be done independently, and that is art, the Arts.

A shoemaker or a carpenter or a manufacturer who is independent is a traitor to his group. Art is the one place where individualism hurts no one. The part of the artist that is a human being is inter-dependent. I am not so foolish as to expect the artist to make an impossible division of himself. But I don't think art is a practical means to a living. To make a living you have to make something that someone else wants. The working-man works for somebody else. He may sell his work to capital or to the government. But in a better world than ours no one will have to sell works of art for a living.

If an artist makes his living as a craftsman, doing commercial work, he must belong to a labor organization that will protect his living. The work he does for himself, his painting, cannot come under the standards of commercial competition.

I question whether you can really be an artist when you have given up your independence. What I am really saying is that the artist who paints for himself is an amateur. In that sense I am proud to be an amateur. So was Rembrandt and so, too, Van Gogh.

I cannot say too strongly how absurd it is to judge whether an artist is good or not by how much his work sells. Selling is a rare consequence of making what happens to be in style largely through the influence of publicity. Pictures that sell may be the work of an artist or just products of some snappy technique. The work of great artists and little artists may sell, you can't tell which way the fashion will turn. The artists who are great today may be of little importance tomorrow. The one who wasn't even called a little artist may eventually be called the great artist.

The dealers, with few exceptions, make a living selling French pictures in the back room. They may show American art in the front room, but they always have a few choice pieces to show their clients, precious things just over from Paris, some rare Cézanne that was discovered in a rubbish heap. Cézanne knew some of them weren't so good and he threw them there. Europe sells us a few things with a tear in her eye and says, behind her hand, "Good riddance for good money!"

There is a museum out in Kansas City. In the will of its patron is a stipulation that no American artist's work can be bought until thirty years after his death. Some of them who die early may get in sooner than those of us who were born before they were. No doubt there are plotters, dealers, preparing to have some pictures ripe when the thirty years are up—or even meditating murder.

Though a living cannot be made at art, art makes living worthwhile. It makes living, living. It makes starving, living. It makes worry, it makes trouble, it makes a life that would be barren of everything—living. It brings life to life.

In a better world everyone will be an artist. Art products will be "swapped." Maybe pictures will be exchanged for somebody's hand-made table or woven textiles or fine pottery. An interest in art will take the place of superiority in wealth. Men will take pride in having hand-made things at a time when the machine supplies all the necessities. Art may come to be the great *desideratum* in a machine world that has abolished hunger and poverty as the result of three hours machine tending per man per day.

Originality and Imitation

Students worry too much about originality. The emphasis on original, individual work in the past years has done a great deal to produce a crop of eccentric fakes and has carried art away from the stream of tradition. Tradition is our heritage of knowledge and experience. We can't get along without it. If we tried to live alone in the woods we would have to start civilization all over again. Humanity would get nowhere without imitations. We would not know how to eat, speak, live without learning by imitation.

[35]

Of what use would language be without imitators? You can create your own vocabulary of word sounds but nobody will understand you. One James Joyce is a miracle but a nation of Joyces would make life impossible.

Art is so much a matter of signs. All phases of creative and plastic art contain these signs. At some time or other these signs were invented or created. If they had been found only in the work of their creator they would probably never have been accepted. It is through the imitator that the significance of signs in the arts is spread to a wider and wider field until many of them are exploited by all ages and all peoples.

An artist who, in years of work, has accomplished only imitations has no need to feel himself a failure. He is, perhaps, working more for the general good in the way of spreading art appreciation than the selfish creative genius. It might not be too much to say that the creative master is a failure until the imitators have found him.

The human ear is a perfect example of what I think about originality. All ears may look alike and yet no two in the world are identical. The convolutions are there in all ears but they are subtly different in each individual.

You can do all the imitating you want, you can respond to anything you choose in life, and in doing that you will simply be doing what the greatest originators among humans have done. Originality cannot be sought after. It will come out when you express your convictions. Never be afraid of losing your individuality. If you have something personal to say you will not be able to hide it.

Originality is a quality that cannot be imitated. The technique of the language, on the other hand, is something that belongs to all who can understand it. Rubens' technique has been in the world so long that it belongs to everybody who can understand and use it.

Sometimes it is best to say something new with an old technique, because ninety-nine people out of a hundred see only the technique. Glackens had the courage to use Renoir's version of the Rubens-Titian technique and he found something new to say with it.

Cézanne may have tried to paint like El Greco, but he couldn't help making Cézannes. He never had to worry about whether he was being original.

Don't be afraid to borrow. The great men, the most original, borrowed from everybody. Witness Shakespeare and Rembrandt. They borrowed from the technique of tradition and created new images by the power of their imagination and human understanding. Little men just borrow from one person. Assimilate all you can from tradition and then say things in your own way.

There are as many ways of drawing as there are ways of thinking and thoughts to think.

Little people with precious techniques, secrets, mysterious recipes for making art, are always chary of sharing their information, because that is all they have. That is not the attitude of a real creative artist. You never hear that one scientist is worrying about another scientist using what he has found out. And yet I had a letter not long ago from a student in Pennsylvania, in which he told me that he had discovered a wonderful method of painting, absolutely new—and he was afraid it would be stolen from him before he could perfect and patent it. What was he to do? I thought of writing him on a postcard, saying, "My dear Sir: I am printing this because I have discovered a new and wonderful way of writing and I am afraid of having it stolen by the postmaster who looks at your mail."

Too little knowledge of technique is a handicap as it holds back what we want to express. The trained hand can control and facilitate the unconscious impulses of the mind.

I can't tell you how to do it. It isn't a secret or I could tell you what it is. The people who make art don't know how they do it.

They don't do it uniformly well. When you "know how to paint" you can be a professional portrait painter than which nothing is more tedious.

Look at the elusiveness and keenness of an artist like El Greco. You may think for a moment that you know how he did it. It isn't as simple as all that. There is a formula that we can see, and then there is something else, some spirit, vision, understanding.

The academicians are the men with little recipes. They learned how to make one picture and they spend their little lives making that same picture over and over again. The masters did have a certain kind of formula, a sort of system in seeing, a method in constructing pictures. That is how we recognize their work. We know a Rembrandt when we see it because we recognize the formula he used, his way of thinking about things.

Know What You Want To Do

You can be a giant among artists without ever attaining any great skill. Facility is a dangerous thing. When there is too much technical ease the brain stops criticizing. Don't let the hand fall into a smart way of putting the mind to sleep. If you were so clever that you could paint a perfect eye, I would know that you would always be too clever. Some things are too well done and not done well enough.

The danger of learning too soon just how you want to paint often results in mass production.

On the other hand, don't be fooled into thinking your work is better than it is because the technique is fumbling.

Be master of your own ability. Work with some confidence in yourself. Work that shows a lack of decision about how the thing is to be seen and executed in the medium betrays a vacillating mind. When you pick up a pencil you are an authority unto yourself. Don't let technique get the best of you. Master it so you can work with more spontaneity and less labor. Skill in expressing what is on your mind is necessary but it takes more than that to make art.

When the work steps forward it is through the use of an ability that isn't always at your command. Keep striving and searching for greater realization. Through that yearning the problems of execution will be solved.

Be sensitive to the qualities inherent in the medium. Paint honestly and avoid tricks.

For a while people thought that putting the paint on roughly was art. Now we know that an artist is a craftsman. It lets in a lot of manicurists.

If there is desire, humanness, and sincerity, even with a fumbling technique a result may be arrived at.

See things your own way. Find out how you, yourself, see things. Do not deceive yourself by following some popular style. If the trend is towards murals do not hesitate to paint easel pictures or miniatures if your concept of things lies in those forms. It is part of mastery to know one's form, one's limitations. Rembrandt did not try to paint frescoes in the grand manner.

If you are most interested in design, perhaps you should not be painting pictures. Rather be a great artist in making pottery or furniture than an unhappy artist painting pictures that do not express your true vision.

Years ago Angna Enters, the great dance mime, came into my night class to finish her equipment for commercial art. I said some things to her that made her think—perhaps something about a feeling that I got from her work that she wanted to express herself in motion as well as line and color. She told me years later that I drove her out of art! With her great human understanding and artistic ability she has created a pantomime theatre that is unsurpassed today. She designs and makes her own costumes, even to dyeing the leather for shoes. She is a great professional artist in the theatre who now paints on the side.

If you are most interested in vivid imagery, it may be that you should be a poet. If you have an intense feeling for rhythm, perhaps you should be a musician.

But if you love to draw, draw. Let it be a means of spiritual communication between you and your fellow beings.

Art and Nature

Nature is what you see plus what you think about it. Artists change our thoughts about nature and so, in a sense, change nature. A masterpiece does not look like nature, because it is a work of art. The language you want to speak is art, so study art from the masters. Nature is made up of things, facts, phenomena. You have to select what you want to make art. It is the job of the artist to correct what he sees by what he knows. Anything you know helps the mind to dominate the eye in seeing. The artist's mental image of the thing seen in nature, expressed in graphic terms, is what gives creative vitality to the work.

Nature: atoms, plants, animals, humans, inorganic things—the whole universe; life around us: cities and mountains, plains and rivers;clouds and sky; the oceans; fire and sunlight; the table and dishes we eat from every day—all is nature: the artist's subject matter. There is no image that was not derived from a memory of something seen. Rembrandt was a great inventor but he has never been accused of inventing or changing nature.

Get your impulse for making a picture from some incident in nature. It may be something about an elbow at a window that tells you all about the room inside.

Every individual has a life of his own and his own concept of beauty. If he responds to those things in life that he has selected as material for creative expression, his work may reach as high a plane as any that has been produced.

The artist should have a point of view, the spectator's attitude about his subject. But he does not need to paint the age in which he lives. They say we should paint the Machine Age, paint speed and change. That is all right if you are interested, but it is not necessary to respond to dynamos and microphones. We have not yet learned to use labor-saving machines to save anything but wages —how then can we paint them with understanding?

The artist seeks to record his awareness of order in life. One may find it in landscapes and another in social themes. The subject may be of first importance to the artist when he starts a picture, but it should be of least importance in the finished product. The subject is of no æsthetic significance.

The average person is satisfied that he understands a picture as soon as he has recognized the subject. If it is a fat,old woman bathing herself, he passes on because he doesn't like her.

The real artist finds beauty in common things. When what you see in nature is obviously beautiful, a picture postcard sunset—then is the time not to paint. Avoid sloppy sentimentality over the obviously spectacular and picturesque. These depend on the color and excitement of the moment. A record of emotions isn't art in any medium, even music. Emotions of a graphic-plastic nature are another thing entirely. The best creative inspiration and stimulation you can get is the tempting impossibility of expressing by signs the third-dimensional realization of Things.

Paint what you know and what you think. Keep your mind on such homely things, such deep-seated truths of reality, that there is no room for the superficial. Put over the selected viewpoint of the mind about the subject. Don't be afraid to be human. Draw with human kindness, with appreciation for the marvel of existence. Humanism can be applied to drawing chairs and cobblestones. Look at the work of Daumier.

There are no superiors among masters, but we may distinguish between the work of Michelangelo and Rembrandt by saying that the latter was more human.

A concern with the abstract beauty of forms, the objective quality of lines,planes,and colors,is not sufficient to create art. The artist must have an interest in life, curiosity and penetrating inquiry into the livingness of things. I don't believe in art for art's sake. I think that very often a literary motive may inspire the finest art, in fact almost always. But the literary title might better be destroyed or kept for the artist's autobiography. If paintings were designed as Opus 1, 2, 3, etc., they might receive more attention from the public.

I sometimes wonder what is to supplant religion in stirring up works of art. Look at those Russian icons! But I don't know why it might not be possible to get that same sort of thing in a painting of bits of human joy in life. I know of a little picture by Philip Evergood, card players on a hand car, that looks like a religious painting.

The purpose of subject matter is to veil technique. The great artist uses the cloak of resemblance to hide the means.

If you want to make great art paint a common thing. The difference between a head drawn by a naïve artist like Rousseau and one drawn by Rembrandt is that Rembrandt drew with greater significance (the use of signs) and understanding.

Draw the things that interest you, that you like or dislike. Many great works of art were motivated by the artist's hatred of the thing drawn. Goya's *War Series* is an example. But in the finished work you do not feel that he hated life and human nature. Work which only conveys the emotion of dislike remains caricature or propaganda.

CHAPTER IV

THINGS—THE MAINSPRING OF ART

AN INTEREST IN THINGS is and always was at the root of art. Giotto painted things. He didn't draw them the way Michelangelo did but they were both after things, the essence of solid forms.

Through the influence of the camera, few artists today know the difference between the aspect and the concept of a thing. It requires mental technique for a student or artist to look at nature and see things. A camera can't see a Thing. It is mentally blind. The camera can't see form. If you see form in a photograph, your mind put it there. We don't even learn form through the eyes. We learn it from the sense of touch. The first two years of a child's life are spent in coördinating the sense of touch with the visual impressions of things seen by the eye. We recognize the shapes of objects by experience, knowing that certain combinations of tones, light and shade effects, indicate shapes of which we have a tactile knowledge.

The eye is only a lens. Triangulation, looking with two eyes, gives a greater sense of the third dimension than can be seen with one eye. If you look around a room with one eye shut you lose your sense of space. You will see just flat color facts. But if you look at a good picture with one eye it has just as much form as can be seen with two eyes because the form is signified, made by signs.

The art schools of the last hundred years have taught students to imitate the visual impression of the light and shade shapes seen by the eye, with no concern for the subjective, real shape of things. People who have a clean innocence about life and the things they see can't understand the average art student's drawing. A child can't. A few years ago an Indian shown a photograph could not tell top from bottom.

The ultra-modern movement is a medicine for the disease of imitating appearances. It is a return to the root principle of art: that art is the result of an interest in Things, not effects. They would have laughed at me if I had talked about drawing Things three hundred years ago for they saw only things, not appearances. Ultra-modern art is simply a return to the technique of art, the use of symbols, graphic devices for things. There is essentially nothing being done by it that cannot be found in an El Greco.

Most of the ultra-modern artists are practising, exposing the grammar, the tools of expression. The imitators are very useful because they spread the technique. The only value of the Surrealists' work is in its moderate concern with realization, the kind of art existence you find on a much higher plane in Dürer or Mantegna. The literary associations in their work are of no importance to anyone but the artists themselves. Or are they? Sad if true.

The stumbling block in modern art is that the artist becomes more interested in craftsmanship than anything else. Cubism is not art in itself. It is the grammar and composition of art. The ultra-modern movement has made us conscious of the skeleton of tradition.

Not that significant technique is the only important element in art. The old masters' work has the same technique which has been discovered by the modernists, but the masters cloaked it in readily recognizable subject-matter or story telling. There never has been a time when it was not good form to speak well of Giotto, Rubens, and Titian, but we have not been conscious of why they were good. It used to be quite possible to look at their work and see only the subject and design,—what might be called the beauty of the work, or its emotional content,—and not be at all conscious of the technique. In fact, it is one of their achievements. In the light of modern investigation, however, such absence of understanding is no longer possible.

Avoid imitative painting, the copying of light shapes and shadow shapes. But this does not mean being alienated too far from representation. Work which is purely non-representational loses some of the texture of life. Students cannot have too much training in cubism but there has to be an interest in life before the work takes on a healthy creative vigor.

The Separation of Form and Color

At the root of all the plastic arts is the consciousness of forms made of combinations and modifications of the universally understood simple solids: the cube, cone, cylinder, pyramid, and sphere. The graphic artist projects his concepts of these forms on a two-dimensional surface by the use of line, tone, and color devices.

Signified third-dimensional projection is one of the æsthetic elements of a work of art. The attempt to imitate sculpture, modelling as seen in nature, by the use of light and shade planes is of no significance.

Realization, the tactile existence of the form, is another basic æsthetic quality. The definition of the form in its entirety, the character of the material represented, not imitated, gives life to the art form created. Realization comes through a feeling of the bulk and weight of the thing, the bruises you would get if you stumbled over it in the dark. Texture clinches the form, brings it into tangibility.

Another point that lends realization to the work of art is the artist's consciousness that form and color are two separate things. The mind cannot sense form and color at the same time. They do not actually happen in anybody's mind at the same time—there are two efforts. The mind registers back and forth very rapidly from form to color. It may make the change a hundred times a minute. Only the mind sees form. If form exists at all it is only in the mind and as the result of experience gained through touch. Color is a surface texture on the thing. We do not understand form through color but through the indications of lights and shadows. If we saw form through color we might mistake a persimmon for a tomato.

The great black and white draughtsman, the sculptor, and the blind man know that form and color are separate. The form itself is what the blind man knows about the thing. Color is a surface skin that fits over the form. Many great works of art have only form, the sculpture of the thing. Color as used to signify realization by men like Titian and Rembrandt, gives greater life and tactile existence to the work.

Realization is the keynote of the Renaissance. Rubens was a master of form and color. He had a formula for making realization, which belongs to any artist who can understand it. Rubens' technique belongs to everybody. It is Rembrandt's and Renoir's. People criticized Glackens for using Renoir's technique. Why not use a traditional technique if you have something of your own to say? Renoir's technique is the technique of tradition, of the separation of form and color.

Because Glackens is a contemporary whose work has been neglected by most critics on account of a surface resemblance to Renoir's, I want to make a special point of the real technical relationship between Glackens and Renoir. Both men worked on the principle of the separation of form and color, which is the technique of tradition. If Glackens is like Renoir, Glackens is like Rubens, Rembrandt, Titian. The same technical principle of plastic realization is in the work of all those men. Of course you won't mistake a Renoir for a Rembrandt. But if you don't recognize the resemblance you don't recognize the principle. People, critics with the "art student" mind, recognizing the superficial technique of Renoir, see only that and pass on.

ILL Pending 19981019

CAN YOU SUPPLY ? ▲YES ▲NO ▲COND ▲FUTUREDATE ¶

▲ :ILL: 6094161 :Borrower: FPR :ReqDate: 19981016 :NeedBefore: 19981115

:Status: PENDING 19981016 :RecDate: :RenewalReq:

:OCLC: 563947 :Source: OCLCILL :DueDate: :NewDueDate:

:Lender: *CYC,PSM,DRB,NHM,CKM

:CALLNO: ¶

▲ :AUTHOR: Sloan, John, 1871-1951 ¶

▲ :TITLE: Gist of art, AD1135.55

▲ :IMPRINT: New York, American artists group, inc. [c1939] ¶

▲ :VERIFIED: OCLC ¶

▲ :PATRON: CERVO,NATHAN ¶

▲ :SHIP TO: ILL/Franklin Pierce College Library/Rindge, NH 03461 ¶

▲ :BILL TO: same ¶

▲ :SHIP VIA: Library Rate :MAXCOST: @N/$0 :COPYRT COMPLIANCE: CCG ¶

▲ :BORROWING NOTES: We do not charge for loans or photocopies(up to 30pp.) Can
you reciprocate? Thank you. ¶

▲ :LENDING CHARGES: :SHIPPED: :SHIP INSURANCE:

▲ :LENDING RESTRICTIONS: ¶

▲ :LENDING NOTES: ¶

▲ :RETURN TO: ¶

NOV 19 1998

If what you mean by technique is only a superficial thing, how the paint is put on canvas, that is nothing. If Glackens' work had not been identified with that of Renoir, if he had imitated the prevalent Munich technique of the 1890's, Duvenyck for instance, no one would ever have called him an imitator. Glackens learned something from Renoir about how to think in paint, but anything he painted was his own. We all need direction to find our way to some relationship with the stream of art. Some imitation is absolutely essential. We catch up with the conduct of today by imitation.

There is no use in trying to be strictly original. All you need to be is honest, and you will gradually reach the conclusion that the world around you isn't real enough to be worthwhile. You soon find that what you see is not real enough to put down. Glackens, like Renoir, worked from a mental concept of the thing itself.

Glackens was a great colorist because he used color as a plastic force. In his work you can see the neutral colors weaving together to build the form, and then the positive colors put on as separate statements to give the form color-texture. The technical process resolves itself into a separation of the color-plastic constituent, from the form. The energizing color-plastic surface is there in his work as in a Renoir, Rembrandt, or El Greco. I, myself, believe that there must be some of this quality that comes from the separation of form and color in any worthwhile work of art. There must be some of it, no matter how simply it is used. If there are only a few lines on a piece of paper there is separation of the form and the color as an enhancing surface texture.

The technique of the old masters was based on that process. They made the form first with light and shade and then the color was fitted over it, and so there is no joining. In the academic work of the last hundred and fifty years there has been no separation of form and color. In a real work of art the form lies under the color, is climaxed by color textures. Put your hand against a Rembrandt of the finest period, when the paint was put on in grooves and scrapes and chunks. Compare the realization in his painting to the flat color of your hand. If you want to make a real test, look at both with one eye. The painting is more real than the hand because the form is realized by Rembrandt's devices, form clinched by color. Perhaps the separation of form and color is more readily recognized in a Rembrandt than in a Renoir. But the principle is there in Renoir and in Glackens.

This related technique which you will find in the work of Titian, in Rembrandt, in Rubens, in Renoir, and in Glackens, is a means to super-realization.

Cézanne was related to this group, although his method was more geometric. Analysis and dissection of the traditional technique is the sub-conscious motive of the whole ultra-modern movement. It is a struggle toward the human, plastic, structural concept of reality which existed in the world to about the time when the camera was invented. The ultra-modern movement is important because it brings us back to a consciousness of the analysis, of the anatomy of things. It brings us back to the artist's concern with the noumenon, the thing itself, rather than the phenomenon.

Things Have Bulk—Art Has Form

The *thing itself* has bulk and modelling. Art has form. If you merely copy the modelling it won't have sculptural impulse. Thickness through doesn't make form. The simple design that is painted around a fine Indian bowl has form. A Chinese painting has no modelling, but form signified, represented by graphic devices.

Form is a kind of slang word these days. Many people think that bulbosity and form are the same thing. There are some who think a form is classical because it is cylindrical.

Of course it is impossible to define good form. The drawing of flat planes, rounded planes, bumps and holes—is only modelling. There must be a sense of organized geometrical shapes, some plan of beauty in the selection, definition and combination of the forms.

One factor that contributes to the fineness of a painting is the limitation of the sculptural quality to low relief. I don't believe there is more than two feet of real depth of space in any great painting. The sense of space is represented by devices. The harmony of sculptured planes is one of the beauties of bas-relief sculpture.

Poetry, music, painting, have form. By form in this sense, I mean the way the artist wraps the thing up and delivers it to the public. It has something to do with manner, style. Imitators may get the form, in this sense, but not the content. They get the stylization but not the true style which is created by the idea. Stylization is just a superficial exaggeration of shapes, a punctuation of decorative qualities.

Style is such a subtle thing that we scarcely see it in the great masterpieces. Style is the finish with which the artist cloaks his thoughts. It is the outside edge of the inner content, the tangible surface of the form. Style is the result of a harmony of concept, a selective force that is the artist's guiding spirit.

The Archetype

The artist has a mental concept of things in nature; he knows their normal structure and proportions. To this he adds his personal point of view, his selection of shapes and proportions and qualities that interest him as being fundamental and beautiful. This mental formula for a thing is called the *archetype*, and it is the basis for comparison to which the artist refers when observing a particular thing in nature.

The artist formulates his idea of the average structure of human beings, trees, mountains, horses, dogs, and so forth. He develops a system of thinking about the general construction of things which makes it possible for him to observe the particular, record it if it interests him, but always as a variation of the norm type.

Archetype thinking may be observed in the work of all the masters. It contributes to the monumental, permanent character of their work. It has a lot to do with the unity and integrity of their concepts. It keeps what we used to call "character" out of great work.

The people in a Daumier or Breughel all look as though they belonged to one family. It is this formula by which we know that a picture is the work of a certain artist or school.

Just as the artist develops some structural system in seeing forms, he works out formulas for expressing them. He uses formulas and systems of drawing and design to express his feeling for order. Discipline of thought and technique are essential in creative work. "The artist must have a heart of fire and a mind of ice."

The Approach

There is no one way of drawing that is right. Nor is it good to be dependent on any one way of doing things. The greatest masters were always searching and groping toward more powerful, significant form, forcing the technique to suit their desires. Delacroix's Notebooks are full of observations about the problem of finding a better way to say what he was after.

Go to the masters to learn how to draw and paint. Study them, particularly the work you don't like. That is the road to advancement, that is the way to learn. But get your impulse to work from life. You may copy Cézanne or El Greco, but whatever you make will be your own. Whatever I make is a Sloan, no matter whose technique I may borrow.

Study and work and paint pictures. You cannot paint pictures by merely wanting to paint them. All the inspired work of the masters is backed up by a lifetime of hard study. Find your own way of working. You may work three hours a day, or fifteen. You may work steadily or only when you feel like it, but it is best to get in the habit of working regularly.

FORM: *Light and Shade*

THE CUBE: *Form, Texture, and Light*

BLACK AND WHITE TEXTURAL PROGRESSION

Light and shade (form)

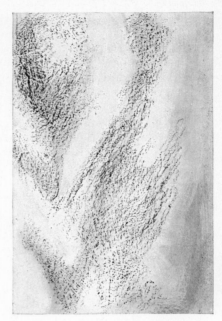

Plus texture in the light

Light increases with color-texture

Linear graphic additions

THINGS—THE MAINSPRING OF ART

It is good consciously to study the devices of drawing, to practise methods of painting. This knowledge must become part of your subconscious equipment or it will bother you when you are trying to create. Make laborious studies to find out how things are made in nature and to increase your technical ability. But do not be afraid to loosen up and have a good time making a picture. When you make a drawing for fun it is apt to be good because you are not hampered by the idea of making Art. In a good drawing you make use of all the information and ability you have been storing up while studying.

An artist who just wishes to paint with nothing in him to paint from, remains an art student all his life. He depends on schools and teachers, and learns methods and manners. The real artist needs no teacher. He will find a way to draw or paint if he has the urge.

Have the courage to make mistakes. Believe in yourself. Learn to be your own teacher and critic. Go to the masters to learn how to do the things that trouble you.

There is a healthy condition in the art student when he starts to create pictures and still goes on studying and assimilating. The important thing is to get the creative urge stirred up, to find out what you want to say about life. When you have that purpose you can go on studying for life.

Almost anything you study may be useful to you as an artist: music, geometry, bricklaying, anatomy, botany. But don't get side-tracked into too much scientific research.

Great art lies somewhere between naïve and intellectual art. Art is not the result of pure reason. There must be some feeling, emotion, excitement about life. Pure abstraction isn't art, it escapes from life. The trouble with Egyptian art is that it is too abstract, too much an art of mathematics, death. The human mind cannot grasp an idea unless it has texture, the texture of living existence.

Setting out to do what ultimately cannot be perfected is what makes art. The effort to do the impossible leads to creative work. It is impossible to paint every leaf on a tree. Trying earnestly to do so results in a creative symbol, as in Rousseau.

Some of the greatest artists' work is full of faults. Those faults have something to do with their greatness.

If you go out for beauty, what will you get—something sweet and innocuous. I strongly suspect that if you go out for realization you may get beauty. Not always, but I think that is the right approach.

There is work which annoys nobody at all, and there are people who pass through life without ever irritating anybody. The kind of work they do is practically faultless to everyone, and consequently enormously stupid. It has that certain degree of slimy innocuousness which is necessary in work that has to pass the opinion of fifteen or twenty voters.

Those paintings are just oil painted documents in handsome gold frames. They win prizes. But what does such a picture have to say. It seems to say, "Aint nature lovely?" But all it really says is that J. Stuntjoy Smythe was in Montauk Point in June; and nature was pretty; the sun threw purple shadows north-northeast. That kind of picture is eating space wherever it is, even in the cellar.

The academic art class takes students and teaches them how to make bad drawings. After they can make perfectly bad drawings, (it takes quite a while to learn how to make very bad ones), they are graduated. They get studios and make bad paintings. The more they paint, the worse they get. If you ask one of those men where their drawings are they will tell you that they are "out of drawings." No one ever heard of a great artist who was out of drawings. Rembrandt was drawing twenty days before he died, so he could paint better.

CHAPTER V

DRAWING

DRAWING IS THE CORNERSTONE of the graphic, plastic arts. Drawing is the coördination of line, tone, and color symbols into formations that express the artist's thought. Drawing and composition are the same thing. They can't exist separately. The artist sees order in life, that is one of the important things he has to say about it. To formulate his visual images he must have order in his thinking and order in his expression. A sense of the structure of things, of their geometrical composition, the ability to see order in nature—and then the technical ability to compose these plastic ideas, is essential to the artist. But if you go out and see nature through a formula of composition you won't go very far.

By the graphic means of line, tone, and texture are made symbols for third-dimensional activity; for form and space, and light and shade.

The line drawing of a cube is a racially accepted symbol for spacial activity. Because it is a sign it is more vital than the reality. A squashed circle is a symbol for the top of a cylinder seen in perspective. It explains the objective character of the form better than an ellipse, which is only the visual appearance of the thing. A set of radiating lines drawn around an object say "light" more powerfully than anything else because it is a sign-convention.

Graphic symbols, devices, are the tools of the artist just as word symbols are the tools of the writer. Study them while you are young, digest them. Men like Picasso and Braque are working for you and me, exposing the technique.

[53]

Drawing has a permanent advantage over all the other methods employed by the artist. When you take a black pencil or crayon and make marks on the white surface of a sheet of paper in order to express something you have in mind, you are using an instrument which confines you strictly to the making of symbols.

 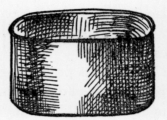

Cylinder Drawn with Visual and Isometric Perspective

If I am a student in a life class and there is a beautiful, flesh-colored model on the stand, and I draw that flesh-colored model with charcoal that is black on paper that is white, I am doing something that has significance entirely as sign-making. Black marks on white paper can never look like that model and therefore, a drawing can never be as bad as an imitative colored painting. The fact that the graphic artist has a means which precludes imitation puts up a barrier between him and a certain kind of worthlessness that can result through stupid imitation of visual sensation without any mental consideration or creative expression getting into the work.

A good drawing has nothing of imitation about it. It gets its value from the quality of invention that the artist has to put into the medium of charcoal or pencil to express what a colorful, living figure suggests to him. We all have graphic courage. When you stop to think that we will put black charcoal marks on white paper to represent a pink figure you will realize that you have lost the fear of dissimilarity. That is one reason why there seems to be a power in reserve in monochromatic work.

DRAWING

Students in the average art academy are encouraged to copy the outlines they see on a model: the high-lights, half-lights, three-quarter-lights, half-shadows, three-quarter-shadows, full-shadows, and the reflected lights,—all in the places where they are seen on the model. That is just as near to black and white photography as they are able to get. It is as far away from art as anything which uses black and white symbols for colored things can go. This putting together of light and shadow shapes has nothing to do with significant drawing.

The instruments of drawing are the pencil, crayon, and pen. Charcoal is a splendid medium because it enables you to achieve so many of the qualities that exist in paint. If there is use for the floating cloud, the blending quality, it is there in charcoal. If there is use for a strong linear signal, it is there. If there is use for the granular textural dryness, as contrasted with the flow of the blended tone, it is there.

The pen is also a wonderful means of intellectual expression in the hands of the graphic artist. The technique of the pen comes very close to registering the mental process of the artist. The pen strikes the paper with its black line. It describes the general contour, the textural contour, the kind of living edge that signifies. It goes further and describes the more important edge, the profile that projects toward you. Then the line follows with textural notations, the roughness of this, the graininess of that, giving a textural face to those vivid creative, expressive contours.

The Attack

You are in class to learn how to draw. But of what use is it to learn how to draw unless you have some real purpose in becoming an artist. Charge your mind with things you want to do, pictures you want to paint. I have heard students speak contemptuously of an artist whose work showed what he "tried" to do. Why, there is nothing more desirable than to have something you want to say and to be able to say it so that you convey your concept to others.

You can't get in the habit too soon of going ahead in a vital way. You need thorough but not dull, academic and mechanical studies to acquire self-control. You must know how to make exact plastic representations of things so you can freely draw your concept of the thing at will. First, good training, then a certain amount of artistic looseness should be your aim. The early works of the masters are quite tight and thoroughly drawn. Later on they loosened up; but having had that foundation of drawing their work is never empty.

The ultra-moderns find it exciting to paint an apple. Let the ultra-moderns find symbols for you and they are yours. Then use them to paint your pictures.

If you are surveying you are not learning how to draw. That is a stupid kind of correct drawing which when mastered would be of no use to you. That is what they teach in our art academies. Really good academic drawing, the result of a thorough training in the tradition of the old masters, is another matter entirely. We haven't had any of that kind of drawing in this country. The reason I wanted an artist like George Grosz on the teaching staff of the Art Students League was because he had had that thorough training in academic drawing. It sticks out all over his work, and yet he can draw like a wise child.

When you draw, your intuition is a sort of guide. You must have a pre-conception in your mind and your hand puts down this concept as if guided invisibly, placing the drawing on the paper as if it were tracing what was already there.

In a good drawing you always feel that the artist chose the ideal place to work from. But that isn't it. It is the feeling of authority which lies behind the good drawing.

Day after day, week after week, you struggle with the problem of drawing freely. Then one day suddenly, the barrier breaks, snaps,—you can draw. You have now become an inventor and are no longer an imitator.

A good drawing has immense vitality because it is explanatory. In a good drawing even its faults have become virtues.

When a drawing is started too quickly it will go on slowly. Work it out mentally for ten minutes before starting; arrange the design in your mind before you put a single mark on paper. If you do that you may be able to put down more, more truthfully and more thoroughly in half an hour, than in a week of stupid, correcting labor. Go after design, character, realization.

Line

Line is the most significant graphic means we have. It is entirely a sign, a mental invention. You don't see lines in nature, only contours of tones. Unless you try to imitate the outside edge of something as the eye sees it, you are making a sign every time you draw a line.

Lines can mean form, depth, shadow and light. Look at the work of the Japanese and Chinese. Notice how the variation of size and strength of the line indicates form and texture.

The line defines the construction of the form, the geometrical shape. The good line does more than describe the outside edge, it contains the form.

The most important outline is an inner line, the contour of the form nearest the person working. The line you would see if you were ninety degrees away from your present position in looking at the thing. This is the "outline of experience," the line that you know mentally about the shape, its projections and recessions.

Think of the line that explains the cross-section of the form. Sometimes draw lines all over the surface, like the lines of latitude and longitude on a globe.

The edge is the consequence of the interior activity. Draw through the form. Reconstruct the shape as you know it. Get at the fundamental geometrical shapes. Try to use line significantly.

Avoid outlines suggesting angular form around bulbous modelling. Keep the line and the sculpture saying the same form.

One ornamental line will weaken every curve in a picture.

There are many line conventions. Parallel wavy lines say water, and they will do their best to say water wherever you put them.

One of the most important line devices is the set of parallel lines used to indicate the surface of a plane, the direction in which it is going and its place. Study the classical line technique of the masters: Dürer, Hogarth, Titian, Leonardo, Rembrandt, and Leech. Observe the system with which they used lines to represent flat and curved surfaces; some to say form, others texture. See how they used lines to say light and shade.

In a Rembrandt there is one line which defines the general shape, then sets of lines that carve the form. On top of this there is a descriptive line which passes to and fro, emphasizing a form here, bringing out the texture there; then the enveloping films of shade.

The fine line is positive and explanatory. It may be as severe as a Dürer or as sensitive and free as a Daumier.

Line is the most powerful device of drawing.

Tone

Unless used to imitate light and shadow shapes, a black tone is purely a symbol. *The tone is a sign for the "thereness," for the presence of a surface.* It may be used to cut in back of a plane, or to pull it forward. A change from light to dark or dark to darker tone indicates a change in the movement of the form. A graduated tone helps to carry a form around. Certain conventions, formulas of tone interval combinations, are devices for making concave and convex surfaces.

Notice how a series of positive tone changes may be used to make the round plane of a cylinder go from front to back. Those tones are signs for surface, they are used to build the solid. They are signifying sculpture, not modelling.

Forms may be built entirely with masses of tone, the boundaries of which make contours. The culminating surface or facet of the form may be a dark or a light. The lightest point of a form does not have to be the most projecting point. It may be struck with a harsh black for the sake of realization or design.

Don't copy the tones you see in nature. The light and shade is only an accident, the real shape is what counts. Study the shape, analyze it into its big geometrical planes. Pick up your tones and build with them. Practise drawing with paint. Mix up a set of positive tones and sculpture with them.

Make many studies of the five simple solids, finding different ways to draw them. Don't rely on one or two little form conventions. Concentrate on the reality of solid substance.

Texture

One of the essences of beauty in graphic art is the *significance of texture*. The signifying of texture, the sign for texture, is what counts. When I put dots and granular markings on the surface of the drawing of a cube, I expose the way to think about texture—not necessarily the way to do it. There are more subtle ways. The texture in a great work of art may be hidden as are other drawing symbols.

Texture is the detail of sculpture. Texture is bulk. Low relief is texture. Pike's Peak and the Grand Canyon are just texture on the surface of America. Texture: All the way from the feeling of a baby's skin to the shape of a chair. The people and easels rising from the floor are the big textures of the floor. The lines of the boards, the spots of old paint and dirt and the general neutral color of the floor, are the minor textures.

Sign-made texture brings the form into sculptural existence, makes it "realized." By realization I do not mean realism. Realism is a kind of fact-painting. *Realization is art existence.* It comes when you make something more real to the mind than it is in nature.

In a Cranach or Dürer every knuckly detail shows an appreciation for something not seen by the eye. It was their way to realization to find warts and hairs, wood-grain, grass, and pebbles to give surfaces textural life. A Titian is so inscrutable that you can't see how he did it.

If you haven't a sense of realization, if you haven't the strong desire and yearning to make things on your paper that will satisfy the mind, you won't go very far as an artist.

Find tones, marks, textures that will clinch the sense of "thereness." Have them at your command, so that when you find yourself losing the feeling of realness you can strengthen your statement and thereby bring it up into existence. Don't depend too much on the textures in nature to keep your sense of reality alive. Exaggerate.

Keep the unity of surface. The surface completely covers the bulk of the thing. Keep your sense of substance alive. Try to make the form tangible. Earnestly scrutinize your own hand with two eyes, then look at your picture with one. Describe the difference between bone and fat and muscle and cloth. Don't do it imitatively by copying the kind of tones and highlights you see. Use the character of the material as a point of departure for some significant statements of what you feel about it.

There are carving textures and color-textures. In a black and white drawing, color-texture is made with selected tones, textures or linework that suggest the surface of the whole form. It is not necessary to put texture all over as though you were embroidering the surface. It may be done with delicate crayon tones, or pushed to the full gamut of black charcoal.

Smeared tones deny existence. Filling-up tones are not texture makers. Texture is drawing the form with more realization than can be achieved by merely describing the plain sculpture of the thing. Melodramatic technique, sloppy oil paint or scribbling pen work do not make the dry existence of the thing—the kind you can get with a few harsh charcoal marks.

You may start the drawing with some nebulous rubbed charcoal grays or water color wash, and then bring it into forceful existence with crisp pen lines and rough dark textures. It may be done with all the sensitivity of a silver point. It may be said in ten minutes with a pencil, or in five years by a very wise painter.

Crude contrasts of black and white do not necessarily make for realization or power. The power that counts is significant drawing. All the greatest work has a combination of strength and delicacy.

Light and Shade

We see what the form is and what it is doing by means of lights and shadows. No matter what the light is doing on the form, the form remains the same. Light cannot obliterate or destroy the shape and weight of the thing itself. We can see that the thing exists, its shape, easier in the light area than in the shadow area. The eye can focus on a light area more easily.

Use the lights and shadows you see in nature to help you define the form. You may follow the light and shade very carefully, or you may pay no attention to the disposition of lights and shadows, in your drawing. But you must plan the light in your design. Light and shade is a device whereby you control the composition of the forms. Use it to carry the eye through the picture, to lead the observer in and out of the design. Decide how you want the large planes to come into the light, and let the modifying planes follow in the same scheme.

Don't just get a record of where the light was in nature, but of what the light did, what its quality was. Use light to emphasize the plasticity of the design. Let some forms slip away into the shadow and bring others up into greater realization.

Rembrandt's drawings are not pictures of lights and shadows. No group of people could possibly be arranged and lighted to look like a Rembrandt. He designed with light. He blessed the composition with light and shade. Someone has said that he orchestrated his lights and shadows.

I like to separate drawing into two processes. First, we sculpture the thing with light and shade, make the shape; and then we bring it into realization with color texture. It may be done by drawing the form with little or no concern for the light and shade in nature. Then with signs, an indication of shadow back of a form here, some textural comments in the light there, the thing can be brought to life. The power of the sign is so great that you can put the very darkest marks in the light, strong granular markings working on top of white paper, and if the shadow side of the form is indicated with a rubbed tone that says shade, those dark marks will stay in the light.

Light and shade don't obscure. They don't cover up the form. Rembrandt's shadows are never dark: they are so full of light that you can always see the form in them.

The color of the thing keeps on going in the light. It is attached to it, an integral part. It is the continuous surface that goes around the form. Don't give up the light area of your drawing to blankness, chalkiness, because it looks that way. Make the thing realized, it helps the sense of light. Avoid keeping your lights too much separated from your darks. Keep them working together. The artist may think of the light side and the shadow side of the form, but he should think more of the thing being enveloped in light and shade. It is a good idea to think, not of light and shade but of light and less light.

Decide on a formula for the light and shade in each drawing and stick to it or the design will become cluttered up.

Some textures reflect more light than others. A black velvet drape absorbs a lot of light. But you know that there is just as much light on it as there is on a flesh-colored model standing in front of it; the light makes it black. Don't be carried away by the contrast of values you see in nature.

Study Daumier's drawings. See how he expressed the feeling of light playing over the form. See how he used light and shade to design. In the hands of a master, light and shade is one of the great qualities of art.

Observations and Reminders

There is an objective value in all the fundamental forms. Horizontal and vertical lines have stability. Diagonals and curves express movement. A circle or spiral gives a feeling of continuous movement. Squares and triangles have strong architectural character. Each of the simple solids has its essential plastic form. The sphere moves around in all directions. The pyramid builds up. The cone builds up and passes around. The column of the cylinder combines the form of cube and sphere.

The fundamental principles of constructing form can be learned from drawing the cube. When you draw a sphere think of it as having a projecting nose, a front corner and then sides, top, bottom and back. Think of the curved surface of a cylinder as having front and sides. Perhaps think of it as a solid octagon or pentagon.

In defining form look for the major flat planes and the major curving planes. If you are drawing a road, the main form is flat modified by static textural surfaces. If you are drawing an orange, it is a sphere first of all, but look for the flat places in it. Find corners, facets, on the smoothly curving ball that will help the mind come to grips with the surface.

It is very difficult to make a perfectly smooth flat surface convincing. You have to find textural modifications to make it tangible.

Generally speaking, it takes three changes in tone to create a culmination, to establish a corner. A corner has three sides: two sides and a top. You don't have "thereness", you don't have realization of the form, until you get the top of the corner.

You can't get realization without putting one tone over another except in the very simplest drawings.

When you are drawing think further around the sides of the object than you can see. If you are drawing a cube face on, you can't see both receding sides but you can think them. With drawing you can signify them. Get up and walk around the thing you are drawing. Analyze its construction. Draw from your memory of the whole shape.

One form demands another. If you draw a cube it has to have a place to exist in.

Build around and up to the most projecting or nearest point of the form, cut in back of the far side. You can sculpture with dark or light. With a line it may be signified by a slight relaxing or sharpening of the line. The feeling of sculpture, the to and fro of the form as it passes away on the far side and projects forward to the near corner, is expressed through the power of mental intention, resulting in significance.

Avoid having the contrast of darkest dark and lightest light at the contour of the form. It arrests the sense of sculpture. Where a light form passes against a dark, lighten the dark a little or put a tone on the edge of the light.

Sometimes relax the degree of sculpturing where the form passes out of sight. Keep the projecting forms more realized than the receding ones or they will fight to exist in the same plane.

The greatest feeling of sculptural realization is secured through sign-giving drawing, not through strong contrast of light and dark. If you want to emphasize the light in a picture, put light around the light areas. Contrasts of dark against light destroy the sensation of light on a surface.

Don't forget that every dark you put on the paper is detracting from the lightness of the paper itself. The tone of the paper can be made to look different when combined with other textures. Observe in a drawing that the white of the paper is a different color in relation to some gray washes than it is when broken or traversed by lines and sharp textures.

Keep the textures clear. Don't fill up the drawing with minor texturings that detract from the sense of light and shade. There must be some harmony in the textural descriptions. In many drawings there is a jarring jump between knowingness and naïveté. One area will be drawn with a very wise understanding and another with a more primitive texture pattern. Such work has a look of uneven competence. You feel that the artist stuffed texture into each area meaning to say bulk, but often resulting in junk.

Remember that the power of harmony is usually stronger than the power of contrast. True of repeating good or bad signs.

Perspective

Objects appear to diminish in size as they recede from the eye. A record of perspective is true only when seen from one point. If you walk across the room from a drawing or photograph that is in true perspective, the forms will become distorted. The tracks of a railroad appear to converge sharply. Visually, the top of a square table, which has four right angles, appears to have two obtuse angles and two acute angles. *Anything seen within fifty feet of the eye is obviously distorted by perspective.* A near hand appears larger than one further away. The neck will look as though it were not set half-way between the shoulders. The far side of the face appears narrower than the near side. The ears seem to be set on the back of the head when we look at the full face. The projecting features of a head seem enlarged.

The artist who is concerned with drawing reality, the subjective truth about things, corrects what he sees by what he knows. The old masters drew the neck in the middle of the shoulders because they knew it was there. Notice that you will seldom find a record of perspective distortion in any of the great masterpieces.

Perspective may be used as a powerful sign for indicating the near and far in a composition. When you are drawing a street full of people, if you make all those in the foreground one size, those in the middle distance reduced in size, and those in the background still smaller, the change in scale carries the eye back. This is partly due to the fact that the eye follows similar forms. In the

Visual Perspective and Foreshortening

drawing of the street itself, the use of converging diagonal lines to carry the eye back is a powerful and useful symbol. But the use of perspective in the drawing of the human figure is undignified because untruthful.

Cézanne made some use of isometric perspective. If he were drawing the top of a table, instead of letting the sides taper away, he drew them parallel, and drew the back edge as wide as the front. If you compare the drawing of a segmented cylinder drawn in isometric perspective to the one drawn with visual perspective you can see the difference. The drawing which records the appearance looks like a tapering form, a cut-off cone. The other retains its real bulk and character no matter from where you look at it.

In drawing a projecting or receding object, *foreshortening* rather than perspective is used to signify distance. If you are drawing a figure with the arm extended toward you, reduce the size of the hand until it is its normal proportion in relation to the size of the face. The arm itself will be drawn in a condensed space. Mark off the position of the elbow about half-way between the wrist and the shoulder, as it is in actuality. Decrease the apparent bulk of the forearm, and increase the bulk of the upper arm. The more abrupt the foreshortening, the more you should increase

Visual Perspective, Isometric Perspective, and Foreshortening

the bulk of the far part of the object, to resist tapering and retain a sense of the fullness of the form. The same method applies to drawing a lying-down figure or the drawing of the head itself. Mark off the normal proportions on the side that is foreshortened. Resist the size of the projecting features, and increase the width of receding parts.

There is no scientific perspective in Oriental work. The Chinese have a convention that a picture is read from the bottom up. The things in the foreground are nearest the eye, those in the middle of the picture are further away, and those things at the top of the picture are in the distance. In landscapes they look down on the foreground, out at the middle distance, and up at the far distance. Conventions such as these have a lot to do with the power and vitality of Oriental art.

The vulgar idea that true perspective is a great and wonderful quality in a picture is a fundamental error. There is no such thing as truth in perspective. Visual fact, the record of a phenomenon, is not truth. This is, I think, obvious when you consider that per-

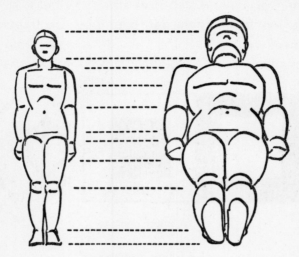

Foreshortening a Figure

spective changes its facts when the observer increases or diminishes his distance from the picture.

Use foreshortening—resist perspective.

Optical Illusions

Optical illusions are of great importance to the artist, particularly the mural painter. In designing a painting to fit in architectural surroundings, lines are greatly influenced by forms outside the picture.

When one plane is superimposed on another, overlaps, there is an illusion of space.

The line symbol of the cube may be seen as a projecting or receding form, solid or hollow, according to its light and shade.

A dark spot on a white surface looks smaller than a white spot of identical size on a black surface. The sensation of light spreads more than dark.

Two lines the same length will appear of different lengths if arrow-heads are drawn on the ends, pointing in opposite directions.

A straight diagonal drawn back of an upright pole will appear to emerge too high on the far side. This is often corrected in Oriental work.

The actual center of a rectangle appears to be lower than it is.

Optical Illusions

That is why we make the lower margin of a picture mat wider to get a satisfactory effect. The capital B is made with the lower loop larger.

When a series of tones are laid side by side, the edge of a light tone appears lighter and the edge of a dark tone darker at the coinciding edges, because of simultaneous contrast.

The effect of yellow seen around a purple spot, known as simultaneous contrast, is an optical illusion. This is a very useful factor in painting, as you can make a color appear brighter than it is by juxtaposing a complementary color.

Design

Composition is based on the law of harmony, the fact that like seeks like. The repetition of lines, forms, tones, and colors is a compelling sign which the eye must follow. Repetition is psychologically pleasing. Contrast is used to emphasize, break up mono-

tony by variation. Contrast and change give a feeling of life, movement, tangibility.

Composition is the coherent organization of forms within a
given area. There can be no drawing without composition. Good
composition is the result of good thinking: some consideration
of major geometrical forms; the balancing of spaces and volumes,
lights and darks, lines, textures, and colors.

Design is an engineering problem. The well articulated design
has the same unity, proportion, and dynamic structural excitement
as a fine bridge. A fine design has scale. It could be reduced in
size or enlarged, and still retain its beauty of measure. This is because of the proportion between the large masses, the minor
masses, and the details. It is compact, yet spacious and easy to
see. It may be comprehended at a glance, and read continuously.

The breadth of decision with which the artist decides on the
dominant rhythms of his design should carry through to the selection of the most subordinate detail. The more complicated the
forms and the more units in the organization, the more planning is
necessary. Without system there is no design.

An artist should be able to take a space of any shape and do
something with it. You can learn much about the principles of
design from the study of geometry and engineering if you are
able to get general ideas without becoming involved in detailed
information.

Design is construction; it is also movement, flow.

Two-dimensional design, the silhouetting of light and dark
masses, is important. But three-dimensional design, the organization of forms, volumes in space, requires more ability. Many artists
should be designing textiles and decorating pottery. Real plastic
design isn't the ornamentation of a flat surface, it is dynamic
construction. If you haven't the creative impulse to work out your
own concept without depending too much on superficial systems
of composition, you won't go very far as a painter.

DRAWING

Some general instructions to be followed or forgotten:

A good design has stability. It is at rest with itself. Sense the opposition of horizontal and vertical rhythms to the dynamic movement of diagonals and curves. Feel the weight of tones and colors; balance and counter-balance them against line and mass.

The center vertical line is an axis, across and around which the rhythms of the design play. You may emphasize a rising movement by using many verticals and pyramiding diagonals. You may emphasize the horizontal by contrast with the vertical, or by the use of many horizontal rhythms.

Base your design on some simple geometrical shape like the equilateral triangle, parallelogram, zigzag, oval, spiral, and so forth. Sometimes I have used letters like A, T, H, N, and others, in working out a composition; or again, I have taken a motif from an Indian design.

All lines tend to keep on going until they are stopped, or continued in another direction by an opposing line or form. Lines that move out of the picture frame must be balanced or checked by others that bring the eye back into the design. A composition that radiates from the center is hard to control.

The eye tends to come to rest at the center of an area. Any form in the middle of the design will tend to arrest the flow of the composition. A symmetrical balance of forms on either side of the central axis of the design will also check the movement. A long narrow space needs to have two centers of interest, held together by some positive rhythm. Veronese often composed with two pyramidal groups linked by a diagonal.

The eye focuses most easily on light areas. When you draw with darks you are emphasizing the light. Any tone that breaks up the continuity of the light hurts the design. Don't misunderstand this to mean no strong color in the light area.

You may design with positively held lines that bind each unit of form. Or you may see in a more sculptural way, subordinating the contours to dominating plastic rhythms. You may use patterns of local color, or subordinate local color to a large light and shade pattern. Goya designed with black and white pattern, Rembrandt with sculptural relief reinforced by light and shade.

In dividing up the areas of a rectangle, asymmetrical divisions are more interesting than even ones, such as dividing a space into thirds rather than halves.

The proportion between the length and side of a space may add to its fineness of measure. As: 2-3, 4-5, 3-5, 5-8, 5-7, etc.

The repetition of a measure always adds to the beauty of the proportions within the space. In Japanese prints you find this done a great deal. For instance, the short length of the rectangle may be repeated in a division of the long space. Or a smaller measure, such as a third of one side, may be used a number of times in selecting the length of lines or position of forms within the design.

A line at right angles to the diagonal is always fine. Squares hidden in the design are often good.

Parallel diagonals (often concealed in curves) give stability and a feeling of unity to the work.

Most of these plans and rules of composition were found by analysis of fine works and are therefore of some importance.

Space

Spacial recession is signified by the graphic device of superimposing one plane on another, the over-lapping of forms. Repetition of forms on a receding plane increases the sense of spacial movement. For example, a set of poles drawn on the surface of a field. Change in scale of similar forms is another sign that indicates the to and fro of space. Planes leading into the picture at a diagonal to the picture plane increase the sense of depth. Reverse perspective or foreshortening gives greater sense of spacial activity than eyesight perspective, because it is a positive sign for projection.

DRAWING

The realization of projecting forms more than receding forms brings about a stereoscopic sensation of space. This is done by the use of tonal intervals, not light and shade imitation of the visual appearance. The use of color recessions gives more power to tone combinations in the black and white scale.

Contrast of texture increases the sense of space, by giving tactile reality, special identity to each form.

If one form is drawn directly above another they will tend to stay in the same plane. This is especially true if they are the same size and the edges touch. If you have one head in back of another, arrange them to overlap so they are not on a vertical line.

If you repeat a background tone or color in the foreground, they may appear to be in the same plane.

Low Relief

A fine composition is like a low relief. If there are houses and people in the foreground, hills and bushes in the middle ground, mountains and sky back of that, there need be only a few inches of modelling between one plane and another. If you look at a Mantegna fresco, you can see that the head of a man in the foreground is only half an inch in front of the mountains that are miles away. The very fact that one thing is superimposed on another is a sign for distance.

Think of the space in your composition as a stage on which no forms may project beyond the proscenium, or picture plane. Plan the dominating spacial rhythms that are to occur, whether they are to run parallel to the picture plane or diagonally into the background. Establish the ground plan. Make it clear that one group of forms is in a certain place in relation to another. Make a place that has front, top, bottom, sides, and back. You may not show a plane to indicate each one of these sides, but think it.

Design with large sculptural planes, chunks of form. Hold things together in groups. Tie the different places in the composition together by forms that pass from one plane to another. It may be done by establishing the surface of the ground with a log or overturned chair; or by the diagonal of a receding wall; or by the gesture of an arm that carries the eye across the space.

If you have forms in the foreground that are cut off by the frame, and not closely related to the objects back of them, they will have a tendency to come out of the picture. This is particularly true if there is a strong change in perspective between the planes. Always hold down the perspective of objects in the front plane.

There should be a harmony of relief in each plane. The sculptural proportions should be unified. If some forms are over-modelled and others held with a very low relief the result is inharmonious, unpleasant. Forms should not project forward of the picture plane, nor holes be cut in the back. Air pockets, atmosphere, destroy the dry sculptural existence of the design.

The form may be sculptured with no more relief than a Giotto, or it may be built as fully as a Rubens or Rembrandt. Both are great. Notice that a Rubens, with all its concern for volumes and spaces, has no air pockets. No forms project in front of the picture plane. The back of the picture is like the backdrop in a theater. The same is true of Tintoretto, Signorelli, Masaccio, all the masters of formal composition.

I like to have a book of Donatello's work around. His bas-reliefs are so full of significant drawing. The painter uses more signs. He can use light and shade to tie planes together, or push them apart. He can use color and pure line. A painting should not look just like a picture of a piece of sculpture.

Composition

Design your page. Don't let things slide casually off the edge of the paper. Establish the large masses of dark and light, the major lines. Fill the whole space. Get the big corners and their modifications so you won't have to put in all the little corners.

Establish the big textural planes. Then go after the details that are vital to those plastic statements.

The details must be thoroughly known whether they are put down or not. A master may leave out the details, but you feel that he knows them and could have put them in if he had considered it necessary to his concept. You can't simplify without knowledge. The naïve simplicity in a Rousseau is the work of a child-like mind. A Rembrandt seems simple because it is a powerfully controlled organization, because he had great feeling and vision of the order of things.

A drawing composed of well-developed details never gets over that look. Get hold of a theme, not just a recurrent chord, a lot of little repeats and variations. Make a living organization. Go after the big rhythms not the embellishment of the theme, just as Isadora Duncan, when she danced, followed the big movements and paid little attention to the lesser ornamentation of the music.

A good composition has its light place, its dark place; a serene area, and an exciting area that is the focal point. The vividly realized parts of the design are set off by foils: flat areas against rich textures; straight lines against curves; holes against projections; halftones against animated darks and lights.

An El Greco, with all its nervous excitement and spacial activity is just as wilfully composed as a Giotto. The solid rhythms are organized, emphasized, subordinated to express movement, and yet the thing as a whole is so stable that no form is out of place. It rises like a flame made of forms twisting and crossing a central axis. But what geometrical understructure; the powerful parallels, the diamonds and pyramids that knit those moving rhythms into a cohesive design unit!

In contrast, the work of Raphael or Poussin is planned with more method, more intellectual procedure. You feel a mathematical order, a severe system in the planning of lines and tones and colors. A system which, when imitated, loses its vigor.

In all great compositions you feel this controlling authority. You feel a reserve of power even in the most exciting designs where the organization seems to be expressed to the full. In a fully realized Rembrandt painting or a pen sketch of five lines you feel that the means chosen were completely adequate, and yet something was said that is utterly beyond the limitation of the technique.

Don't think of composition as something you attend to once or twice a week. Be making complete statements all the time you are working. Composing is a continuous and controlling process. Don't think that you design the composition and then attend to filling in the details. The composition keeps right on going until you stop working. When you are filling in the last eyelash you are still composing, I hope. The final changes, lightening a tone here, sharpening an edge there, are changes made because, in your judgment, they improve the composition.

Keep the drawing unified. Do not use one technique in one area, another somewhere else. If you use light and shade the whole composition must be governed by that. If the design is planned in contrasts of tones, built up out of tonal massings, stick to that procedure. Then changes to linear and textural definition will give variety, but they must be carried out through the whole design in a related manner.

Design with textural realization. Emphasize the tangibility of the forms on which attention is to be focused. Get the feeling that some objects are hard, others soft; that some forms are active, others passive. Decide which forms and textures you want to emphasize. Bring out the character and gesture of the dominant forms. Don't let yourself be distracted from your concept by the many facts in nature.

Put down a positive concept. When you have carried through the fundamental relationships of the design, if you need to make changes, do so. Perhaps start all over again. But get an idea and stick to it. Select the quality you want to express and put it across.

It is a difficult problem to solve the influence of small areas on the rest of the canvas. There may be just one repetition too many of a line or tone that will make the whole design seem monotonous. Just one positive dark too many may destroy the sense of delicacy. Avoid habits of casual repetition. A telling touch will be weakened and its usefulness destroyed if it is used just once too often.

If in a drawing, a water color wash is used to say nothingness in one area, you have discounted the use of that tone to make texture in any other part of the picture.

I have seen students' drawings in which an area might be a corner of the Grand Canyon or almost anything but the foot it was supposed to be. Every part of a drawing should be so explicit as to stand alone, and be recognizable for what it is when separated from the rest of the design.

Get the solid geometry of the form. Avoid doughy construction. It destroys the measurements by which you realize the solid. You should know what a cross-section would look like.

If your sculpturing is mealy it will look moth-eaten, like a quilted fog with buttons ever so often. Get some vitality, some significant measures and positive tone changes to work on. A common fault we get into from going in for some of the modern tricks is to fill a picture with little culminations, little kinks, and no main kink.

A drawing full of units of the same size, scattered pell-mell like playing cards, has no coördination. It is hard to see. You go into it one way and have to stop and then try another. It is like a regularly crumpled surface with all the crumples about the same height and no dominating crumple. That kind of design has a decorative quality which belongs on a textile, not in a painting.

If the symbol of ease and the symbol of sculpture have been going together on a canvas, the symbol of ease by itself will carry a suggestion of sculpture.

There are two ways of drawing. You may start with a definite linear statement of the form, and then work up the sculpture with tones and textures. In the work of men like Mantegna and Dürer you feel that the concept was completed in the mind before the artist touched pencil to paper.

On the other hand a man like Renoir would start feeling for the forms with some nebulous tones; a sort of textural description of the place. Then he would begin to catch hold of a corner here, an edge there; the plastic rhythms would emerge from this under-tone. More drawing marks and clinching textures; a lightening here, a darker note there, until the forms were brought into thrills of culmination. In Rembrandt the two ways of thinking and working are combined. It is part of his mastery. But always there is a separation of the under-thing and the superimposed color-texture.

Crowds and Places

When you draw a crowd of people in a street or room or landscape, decide whether you want to say that the people dominate the place or that the place is more important than the people.

Think of the crowd as a bulk, a chunk of form that has top and front and back. Get the structure of the whole group as a shape, and then describe the shape by saying that it is composed of people. Study the way Daumier and Rembrandt drew groups and crowds. See how they got the gesture of the group. If you go through their drawings you will find many studies of the same group of people drawn from different positions and in different lighting. They drew the same places over and over again until they got a concept that fully expressed this.

A crowd is a mass, with heads, bodies, arms and legs. In drawing a large crowd eighty out of a hundred heads, arms, and legs are of no importance. Don't go in for melodramatic gestures. People don't act like opera singers. Get the character, the gesture of the crowd.

Use the background as a container for the people. Make it solid.

Get the textures of the buildings and ground and sky. Find some
thing to say about the quality of the place, the real atmosphere,
the feeling of light and color. Select details that bring out your
point of view and suppress facts that interfere with the story.

Look at the character of the forms in a Von Ostade drawing.
It may be a sketch of an old barn full of people dancing and eating.
You feel the weight of the things, their textures, their relation to
the place. How monumental the design is without being dramatic!
Just common people in a scene from daily life. No need to draw
parades and assassinations to find excitement in life, to cover up
casual drawing. That man, Von Ostade, knew his material. He was
an observer, appreciative of the things around him.

Look at a Breughel. Notice how he used geometric lines to
lead the eye from one group to another. Ever so often there is a
cluster of figures where some important lines pass and converge,
or an angle turns. Notice how the line that runs through the design
may be picked up by a pile of over-turned dishes or a single figure,
and then pass across a space into a crowd of people—a sort of
interior descriptive line. See how he uses a change in scale from
the figures in the foreground to those in the middle distance, as a
sign for recession. The ground is held simply as a place on which
exist those exciting textures of the people and houses. But above
all, how interested he was in everything. Every detail, whether a
hand in the foreground or a tiny tree on the horizon, is drawn
with understanding and human interest.

John Leech's drawings published in London *Punch* in the fifties
and sixties of the last century deserve careful attention. In line
drawing, I rate Leech the peer of any of the greatest masters.

When art students start to make compositions they habitually
draw inflated bulbous people all blown up to a proper degree of
semi-rotundity. The people in their drawings look like bubbles
all over a piecrust. Go out in the street and see how simply the
figures exist as textures upon the surroundings.

In a composition of an interior lit by a number of lamps, the student's tendency is to make the light sources blank white areas. But the sign for light is not carried out through the composition. You need to put in only a few things about the light, a few well-selected shadows, to give the whole area a sense of light. Just as a background has to afford some plastic support to the figures, so you must have some supporting remarks about the light to carry the light from the sources of illumination. Shadows don't help light in a light area: textural realization in the light, opposed to shade—gives real sense of light. The light and shade pattern is a matter of design.

Just because you were looking down from a window at some boys playing in the street, you don't have to draw them from above. It would do you good to project your mind's eye onto the street and draw them from there. If you do draw them from on top, you must know something about the cross-sections of the forms. Consult the work of the great Venetian mural painters. They could draw things from above and below, any position they chose. Observe the wise foreshortening in their work.

When you have a window in the picture through which you can see the scenery outside, don't let the forms float out of the picture. Don't just toss in any old clouds and hills, as though that part were a piece of someone else's picture pasted in back of the window frame.

There are paintings so lacking in composition, they look as if the artist had been throwing a lasso at nature and had corralled a little information, and had sent out another rope and another—all without any complete purpose or idea. The drawing consequently looks as dull as life does sometimes. Why draw the subject if you can't inject some of your own mental activity into the vapidity of nature as you see it? It is foolish to criticize and attempt to correct the little faults in a poor composition. The real fault is the artist's lack of interest, enthusiasm for the subject.

DRAWING

Purpose

Try to decide why you want to draw. Hamlet and Faust and Algeria were real to Delacroix. He made masterpieces of those subjects. But literary subjects are not to be recommended unless you feel them strongly.

Have a plastic, illustrative point of view about life rather than an artistic one. Draw what you see around you. It may be a corner of your room with a couple of chairs and a cat, or it may be a restaurant full of people that interests you. Make life documents, plastic records about life. Find what is vital, meaningful to you.

I like to see students get the healthy point of view that men like Hogarth and Leech and Cruikshank had. Do illustrations for a while. It won't hurt you. Get out of the art school and studio. Go out into the streets and look at life. Fill your notebooks with drawings of people in subways and at lunch counters. Two women gossiping over a table may be the motif for a picture.

Draw places you have seen from memory. I used to paint things I had glimpsed through windows while riding in the elevated train. Remember the kind of place it was. Get the character of the whole room as well as the human being in it. The sturdiness of a chair, the delicacy of muslin curtains blowing in the window. The tired look of the rug on the floor. The droop of the woman's hand in her lap, the tired folds of her skirt. Get the heat of the room.

Artists find ways to say sound and smell as well as sight and touch. The big artists do.

A sense of humor is not incompatible with being earnest. It gets you over that dull, serious feeling, "Now, I am going to make a composition." To have something humorous to say is a good reason for drawing.

Think of drawing as a way of talking about the things that interest you. The sketches we make in letters are often better than finished paintings because we are not trying to make works of art. You know those wonderful documents, drawings made on scraps of paper by the lesser Dutch masters while they were wandering around market places and sitting in saloons—probably made by men who couldn't read a book.

Criticism and Taste

The trouble with most painters is that they don't start over again often enough. They get an eye or a nose or something else they like, and they don't want to risk losing it. You don't learn much when you work that way because you are just making that happy eye and nose over and over again. Dig into the work. Make a mess of it. Fight with the drawing. Put in everything you know and then eliminate. Make the thing ugly enough to be real.

Draw the same thing over many times. Push the intention through in one drawing or in fifty drawings. I have seen Glackens, that great painter and illustrator, make the same drawing over twenty times because he was never satisfied.

Have a degree of realization that you demand of yourself today. Next month you must ask more because, if you have been working, you will be that much more competent.

If you work along one direction instead of along several, you don't go ahead and so go backwards. Make studies. Make pictures. Make large and small drawings. Work with color. But always keep drawing. Bite off more than you can chew. It keeps you from getting in a rut.

Be sensitive to your mistakes. Observe your work. Put it on the wall for a couple of weeks. It may be that you can learn more from the study of your own work than from others.

Take advantage of where your subconscious mind leads you. Some of the best things in a drawing come unconsciously, intuitively.

Keep an open mind, but not so open that it becomes a dumping ground for everything that comes along.

DRAWING

Avoid things that prevent your sense of criticism from functioning. Melodramatic subject matter and clever visual technique keep the mind from functioning, from being concerned with reality.

One of the main things Henri taught was that the artist and student should be his own critic. If you are dependent on teachers you may lose initiative to judge for yourself.

People of extraordinary taste can't stand their own mistakes. They can't stand their own work while they are learning. They are rendered incompetent by too much critical sense, the wrong kind of critical sense. They are so utterly disgusted with what they do. "Don't look at that," they say; "just wait and see what I am going to do," they imply. These people are apt to find some little way of doing things, with a kind of professional technique. But they can never advance because of their fear of making a messy study.

To most of us it is more important to cultivate the ability to find something good in a work than to find its faults. It is much rarer to have a critical sense in that direction.

Study

Study the masters to learn what they did and how they did it, to find a reason for being a painter yourself. Copy the work of the great masters of form, the men who lived before the camera was invented. Men like Masaccio, Signorelli, Michelangelo, Leonardo, Titian, Rubens, Dürer, El Greco, Daumier, Delacroix, and the others. Find out how they constructed form, how they signified texture and space and light. Find out how they designed—what the process of thought was in building up a composition. Make diagrams in which you explain to yourself how the thing was put together.

Make careful drawings in which you study the articulation of the forms, maybe just an eye or nose or ear. Never copy by imitating the lines and tones, but recreate the thing from the large forms down to the fine delicacy of finish, as it was made by the artist.

[83]

Sometimes copy a thing that is in tone with line technique, translate it into a different symbol. The important thing is to learn something while you are doing it.

Draw a fine piece of sculpture like Michelangelo's *Entombment* in Florence. The thing has three or four faces where it is like a drawing. Look at the planes, study them, then draw your analysis of the thing. It is better to make some diagrammatic drawings than a stupid, realistic copy. Perhaps work the thing out in clay. Get the geometric bulk of the thing.

The Chinese students practise for years. They don't stop practising when they become artists. They are always studying, copying the masterpieces of their great traditional art. They practise the symbols of drawing with the brush for years, striving to achieve the greatest meaning with the most economy of means.

Look at the drawings in Hokusai's sketch books. See how vital and significant the line is. You should know his work. You don't need to use his technique to learn something from him.

When Rembrandt's possessions were going to be sold at auction he was working up until the last minute making copies of his Oriental miniatures so he could have some memoranda of them. They are very beautiful drawings in themselves. But you don't see any mannerisms from the study of Oriental work cropping out in Rembrandt. He had a set of Lucas van Leyden engravings which he studied a great deal, but his work is always Rembrandt.

You cannot study music by going out and listening to running brooks and lowing kine. The way to study art is to look at art. See pictures. When someone asked Renoir which he would take if he had to choose between the museum and nature, he chose the museum.

Sometimes you learn more from an unfinished picture. You can see how the artist was working, what he was thinking about. Look at pictures by the lesser masters. You can observe methods that are hidden in the great works. Don't spurn all the works that the experts have labelled as not genuine. If it is good and you can learn something from it, what difference does it make who did it? There is too much fuss over the name of the artist. Nobody knows who built the great cathedrals, who carved the masterpieces of Gothic sculpture. An artist's signature is only a convenient tag for identifying the work.

Nowadays you can have quite a fine collection of color prints to study. Keep them up on the wall to observe in your leisure time. They are good in the large color relations of the design, but remember that they can never have the real technical characteristics of the original.

I suppose you don't really learn anything when you make a good drawing. It is like the flower of a plant. But a flower is just a flower. A new branch is far more important. Don't get discouraged. You are doing the important work when you are studying. There are a few great artists once in a while, the flowers, but they can't get along without the roots and branches. It is the humble root and trunk and branch that carries on the tradition from generation to generation through the centuries. We are just getting ready for the great artist of the century, the Will Shakespeare of our time who will come along and gather up all the material we have been working on. He may be wheeling around Brooklyn in a baby carriage.

Sketch everything. Pass nothing by because you think it is too trivial to observe. It may be exactly what you will try hard to recall from your memory some day.

Work from memory constantly. Store up information about things. Try to draw some place from memory and you will find how little you really know about it. Observe the construction and proportions. Define in your mind what gave special character to each form. When you remember something you make use of the archetype. You compare what you saw with the type concept you have formed. If a man like Dürer wanted to draw a hunchback, he drew his average figure, and then put a hump on it. The artist should have such complete knowledge that he could draw anything in any position. This ability comes through constant observation of nature and practise in drawing from the imagination.

Look at your drawings in a mirror. It gives you a fresh impression of the work. You can see distortions that are not intended, places in the composition that do not work.

When I have students in my class who have been trained in eyesight drawing and who have too much facility, I recommend that they draw with the left hand. By crippling themselves in this way, they are able to concentrate on the problem of expressing the real form, unhampered by their acquired dexterity.

Carry a notebook with you and make drawings that will be useful for your painting—informatory drawings—maybe the gesture of a couple of hands. The action of people walking down the street; feet in a trolley car; mail-boxes and street lamps; a pile of dishes on a table; the sleeve of a coat hung over a chair; all these are details, studies you should save as material for making pictures. Most important of all is to observe while you are drawing, so that you enrich your memory. Soon you will not need to refer to your sketches.

Such training is essential to the illustrator and, after all, there is an element of illustration in all great art. The work of Daumier, Rembrandt, all the great religious paintings—they were all illustrations.

CHAPTER VI

FIGURE DRAWING

IN GREAT WORKS OF ART the human figure has been the point of departure for an exciting, beautiful design; the motive for plastic design. At least, that is how it seems to me.

Works of art are made of wood and bronze and oil paint, not flesh and blood. I don't like a nude that looks too much like human flesh. I think it might better have a dry, hard look, be sculptured with color-textures like a piece of bronze.

A good figure drawing is a "living wooden image." I sometimes tell students to make wooden Indians rather than to imitate the visual realism of flesh.

Most of the pictures of nudes which people hang in their homes are pornographic. Perhaps this is why so few people buy them.

The important thing to bear in mind while drawing the figure is that the model is a human being, that it is alive, that it exists there on the stand. Look on the model with respect, appreciate his or her humanity. Be very humble before that human being. Be filled with wonder at its reality and life. There is a human creature that lives and breathes and feels, a thing with a mind and character of its own—not a patchwork of light and shadow, color shapes.

Sometimes when I come into the classroom I look at the model and see that she is shivering with cold or suffering in some difficult pose she is trying to hold too long. You look up at her and back at the paper, tick-tock, back and forth—all you are looking for is some detail of the appearance of the figure.

Be kind to human beings. Don't make caricatures. It is easy

enough to be cruel. Find the worthwhile things first. Get the gravity, the strength, the repose of the model. We all have faults—some we were born with—we must try to think graciously of faults in others. You cannot be too human, but do not be sentimental. Be yourself.

The reason Rembrandt and Daumier were greater artists than some others is that they were more human. If you think of a human being when drawing from the figure, you will make much finer drawings.

Try to get some personal point of view into your figure drawing. Anatomical perfection isn't exciting. A thorough working knowledge of anatomy is useful in helping you to realize the human figure. Do some dissection if you like, but remember that you are learning facts.

We should know enough about the figure and have sufficient command over the graphic tools to be able to "write in the figure"; to be able to draw the figure in fifteen or twenty minutes as easily as a writer could tell you that there is someone standing on the model-stand in a certain position.

Get a general sense of the human figure by drawing from life and from memory. Find a practical understanding of the average human figure. Seek an adequate symbol for the figure, its construction and proportions. From this concept in your memory, you can draw special figures, with different proportions of measures and volumes that are the basis of variations in character.

It might be well for the student of drawing to take up sculpture for a while to get a sense of the complete figure, the solid construction of the body. It certainly would be good for sculptors to draw more. Most sculpture is a kind of bad drawing over which you can stumble in the dark.

Study the master draughtsmen and sculptors, from Giotto and Donatello to Delacroix and Barye. Their work has almost no concern with what the figure looks like. Each man had a formula for what the figure is. They differ in proportion and interpretation of structure. Study the work of many artists to learn what they thought about the figure and how they said it.

Accuracy of anatomical fact is not essential. I guess Giotto didn't have an anatomy book, but he had structural understanding. A man like Blake did not hesitate to make up his own anatomy. He is like a man who learns Spencerian penmanship and then writes in his own hand.

Anatomy

Anatomy is the study of the structure of the body. The principles of construction are the same in dog, horse, human. But anatomy is not the study of learning how to draw a certain joint in a certain position—as taught in most artists' anatomy books. Use a surgeon's anatomy, or Fritz Schider's *Plastischer Anatomischer Handatlas*.

Demonstrations of building the muscles on the skeleton with clay are very valuable. This is done in most medical colleges and some art schools. Thomas Anschutz used to do it at the Pennsylvania Academy. He and Eakins were real students of anatomy. They did a great deal of dissection. The trouble with dissection is that you work from the superficial muscles to the most important ones. When you see the figure built up in clay by a good lecturer, you get a better sense of plastic structure and function.

You have to know about the interior construction of the bones and muscles that support the figure. In the drawing it is only necessary to show the muscles that make important changes on the surface forms. The point is to have a sound knowledge of construction and function so you could draw the figure without the model.

The more anatomy you know and the less your work shows it the better. If a knowledge of anatomy is all your drawing shows it might just as well be a sheet of paper covered with chemistry symbols. Don't let anatomy ride you, correct it by humanness.

Proportions

In starting to study it is more important to learn the average construction and proportions rather than the particular. It would be well if an art student could spend some time sorting out bones to learn their proportions and character; to gain a sense of the size of the head to the hand and foot; the lengths of arms and legs; the sizes and articulation of joints.

The height of the figure is roughly the same as the distance from fingertip to fingertip when the arms are outspread. The middle of the normal figure is at the junction of the pubic bones.

The head is contained in the average figure about seven times. The Greeks often used the proportion of eight heads to the body which lends a fine sensitivity to their work.

The foot is about the same length as the height of the head. The hand is about the size of the face.

The eyes are set in the middle of the head. If this proportion is changed it is very noticeable. From the chin to the nose, the bottom of the nose to the eyes, and from the eyes to the top of the forehead, are generally equal. The ears are usually the same size as the nose. Notice the unpleasantness of a very small ear.

From the apex of the chin to the outside of the eyesockets can generally be set in an equilateral triangle. By wilfully disturbing this you can change the apparent size of the head and determine the type of face.

It is possible that a very fine sense of proportion is all that an artist needs in the way of taste: Like knowing whether the distance from the lower lip to the nostril is longer than from the nostril to the eye. A fineness of measures in the two-dimensional proportions is important, but plastic proportions, the quality of volumes, is much harder to get hold of.

No great work of art ever contained accurate dimensions. There are no sure rules for fine proportions. Every work of art has its own wilful, harmonious measures. El Greco may have distorted the normal proportions of the figure, but he carried out his point of view all through the forms in the design.

We study the human figure because it has fine proportions, beauty of construction and probably because we are human. We may decide to paint landscapes, still lifes or animals, but we find the greatest understanding of beauty of form and proportion from the study of the human figure.

Anatomical Facts (to be remembered, if possible)

The spine is the axis of the bony structure, to which are attached the rib cage and the pelvis. The neck is set in the middle of the shoulders, no matter how it may look in perspective. The bilateral construction of the body is important to remember when you see visual distortions. Both arms and both legs are the same size. The features, eyes, ears, on opposite sides of the face are the same size.

Study the bones and the joints. Build the figure from the skeleton out, with those muscular supports which vitally interest you in the action of the pose.

Learn the shape of the rib cage; the set of the pelvis, its function as a supporting base to the contents of the torso. Notice which parts of the spine are movable and why: stiff where it becomes part of the pelvis, free in the lumbar region, stiff where the rib cage is attached, and then movable in the neck. See how the head is set on top of the spinal column with a kind of swivel joint.

Learn how the hip joint fits into the pelvis. Study the model when he is standing on one leg and again with the weight on both legs. The hip joint is a ball and socket joint, similar to the shoulder. Study its rotation.

Learn how the clavicle and scapula function; see how the arms are hung onto the body. Find out how the radius and ulna rotate. Draw the wrist joint, the bony mass of the hand, the delicate joints of the fingers. Get into the joints. You can't know too much about anatomical construction so long as you are master of the knowledge. Don't be overwhelmed by the facts. They are tools, sources of information you draw on to express something you want to say about life.

The knee is a joint. If you were a clever mechanic you could build one, take it apart and put it together again. Draw to say that you understand how the thing works.

The foot is built like a bridge; it has a function, to support the figure. It is made of bones and joints and tendons, not putty. The toes are the consequence of the muscular outfit of the feet. If the toes look as though you had counted them in your drawing there are sure to be too many.

Draw the skull. Really study it. Know it from the front and back and top and bottom. Go to a Natural History museum and study the skulls of different races. See the difference between oriental and occidental faces; it is in the skull.

Look for the structural continuity in the figure. The bones are the support to the muscular system; they do not support the weight of the body. The body is held upright by the tension and balancing of opposing groups of muscles.

Every time the position of the body is changed, there is a redistribution of weights to keep the figure in equilibrium. For instance, when the weight is on one hip the opposite shoulder is raised and the spine is curved in the lumbar region to accomodate the asymmetrical balance of rib cage and pelvis. The figure is a series of weights balanced around a central axis. When the figure is resting at ease on one leg, the back of the neck is always on a vertical line with the arch of the foot bearing the weight.

Study the balancing of weights as the model walks around the room, the opposite arm thrown forward to the leg in advance. The body keeps composing itself.

Drawing is a matter of articulation. You can learn a lot about it from the study of the human body. Notice the opposition of vertical and horizontal forms, the branching of arms and legs from the torso, the fitting of solid into solid at the joints. Look at the sequence of forms, as the fullness of the forearm tapers to the wrist, and the spread of the hand into fingers.

Study the big muscular forms. Learn the more important ones first and don't try to concern yourself with modifying actions until you have grasped the fundamental ones. Think of the muscles as groups of contracting and expanding rubber bands. Notice how they act as levers with the bones for fulcrums.

Find the function of each great muscular system. See the way the arm is attached to the trunk by muscles, from the neck all the way down the spinal column in back and to the rib cage in front, as well as by the bony joint of the clavicle. Almost all the muscles of the trunk belong to the arm. The long supporting muscles of the torso hold the body erect, and pull it forward, back, and sideways. Study the fan-shaped attachment to the pelvis of the leg muscles that swing the body and legs in walking.

Get the attachment of the hamstrings to the condyles of the knee; the tension of the Achilles tendon. All the muscles of the calf belong to the foot. The bones and pads and muscles of the foot are arranged as shock absorbers, to keep the body in equilibrium when in action, and to hold the weight. Notice which muscles show on the surface when the foot is flexed, extended, rotated. Learn those little things such as which side of the ankle joint is higher.

Solve the leg. Curves are the result of structure. The curve of the leg is just the outside edge of the bony support and its superstructure. If you know anything real about anatomy, about the skeleton, and the continuous organization of the muscles, you won't draw the figure with a lot of bulbous curves. If you don't want to use your mind enough to learn about the structure of the human figure, or if you haven't got that kind of a mind, draw something else. Or if you must draw the figure, think of it as a

series of cubes. It is better to think of it as a series of cubes modified into cylinders than to think of it as cylinders first.

Study the bones of the hand, the bony mass that makes the
curve and shape of the palm. Draw the bones of the fingers; get
familiar with the character of the joints. Think about the wrist.
Find a sign to say that the arm joins the hand at this point. Never
mind if it doesn't join your way in the anatomy book, make a
joint. Make a wooden joint first and after a while you will learn
how to make a more complicated living drawing. Leave out the
little bumps and dimples and hollows until they mean real structure to you. When you know more about anatomy you can draw
the construction of the wrist from the inside out. And then when
that knowledge has become part of your subconscious equipment,
you will be drawing the wrist without thinking about how you are
making it.

Don't just bat out four fingers and any old thumb. Some hands
are square, others like flames. Fingers may be blunt, curved, angular.
The hand is a very human thing, like a little animal. It can
tell a great deal about the person. There are working hands and
delicate hands. Each finger is different, even the fingernails have
a characterful shape of their own. The form and curved plane of
the fingernail belongs to a particular finger. You may draw the
whole finger with two lines, but you must have sensed its complete
structure. Even if a hand is fat draw it firmly. Find something
to say that will give it the texture of a human thing.

The head is first of all a cylinder, set on the column of the
neck. Think of the nose as a pyramid or half a cone. The mouth
is the surface texture of a large form, a truncated cone that passes
into and under the cheekbones following the line of the jaw; the
jaw, a triangular bone with upright wings attached under the
cheekbones. This is the only free joint of the head except where
the skull is attached to the spine.

Study the big shape of the skull. The curve of the back of the cranium. See how the forehead moves into the temples and joins the brows. The eyes are two spheres set in the eyesockets. Learn the articulation of the muscles at the back of the neck and those which attach the head to the clavicle. Notice how the shape of the neck changes when the head is twisted. Study the big trapezius muscle that is attached to the back of the skull, the scapula, and the spine. Get the muscular formation of the jawbone, watch it while someone is eating or singing.

The features don't make holes in the skull. They happen very simply. They are the natural consequences of the structure of the head. The face is just part of the big plastic form of the head. Think of the features as textures on the surface of a cube. They may be very complicated, but keep them subordinate to the head itself; keep the low relief concept plain.

The eyes are set deeper beneath the brow in men than in women. The male skeleton is more angular than the female.

I solemnly swear that all the above facts are useful to the artist. I also depose that they are better relegated to the sub-conscious, after serious study and practise.

The Pose

Pose the model so you can see the sculptural geometry of the figure. In class you should have a variety of standing, sitting, and lying-down poses so that you can become familiar with the structure of the body in different positions.

North light is best to work in because it shows up the serene structure of the forms with a minimum of accidental shadows. Remember, however, that the light and shadow shapes you see are not the thing itself. If the model were surrounded by equally strong light on all sides above and below, no shadows would be visible. The model would still be there to draw.

If there were some way of having the model-stand turn around or else to have light move around the figure, you could see that the shadows are not part of the figure, but only lie on it. If the stand turned around, you would have to form a mental image of the whole pose, and then decide on one view that you wished to draw.

Most students can't tell you what pose the model has been holding in the last half hour because they have been so concerned with the way she looked. Understand the pose. Take the position, yourself. Walk around the model and see what is happening on the side you can't see.

Find some line of gesture, some plastic ridge in the pose that interests you. Have an architectural, dynamic reason for drawing.

Draw the figure as a set of blocks jointed together. Get the axis of the pose, the balance of weights. Get the character of the big proportions. Make a drawing a day that way for months.

Think of the figure as a column, a solid octagon. It has a front face, sides, and the sides that pass around out of sight, and a back. It has a top and bottom. It has weight, it stands on the ground.

Get into the pose. Feel the strain of muscles. Don't take it so easy. You should feel as tired as the model is when you are through working. Get the relation of the supporting leg to the spine and pelvis, the shoulders and head. Draw the neck in the middle of the shoulders, even in the profile view. Make both legs and feet the same size even when one is far away from you.

Think of the figure as a solid, a modified column of bulk, surrounded by light. Set it up on the model-stand like a monument. Get the rise and positive gesture of the pose. Carve it from that upright cylinder you have established on the paper.

Pretend sometimes that the model is a bunch of sticks, and bend it into different positions and groupings.

The big design of the body is texture. The muscular sculpturings, features of the face, fingers, toes, breasts, are just minor textures. Support the plastic existence of the figure by finding some spacial recessions that interest you in the background. Perhaps begin by putting in the corner of the model-stand, then a few marks for the floor to give the stand a place to be. Then the back edge of the stand and the walls rising and passing back of that. Don't make holes back of the figure; find "thereness," make plastic comments about some corners in the background. Corners, projections, recessions, that will support the figure.

Get the floor there. Establish the plane and then give it surface, texture. Do it with the boards, do it with the smudges of paint on it, do it with a shadow, if you wish, but get it there. Put in a box or a pair of shoes to give it place and interest. Make it say floor, something that furniture can rest on.

At times add something to the pose that will give it more the look of everyday life than the art-school-pose-look. Put in the corner of a bed or some furniture or part of a room. Be making pictures and compositions; add something to the pose beside those miserable draperies hung on the screen. Use your imagination. Make a place. Put in something to tell a story.

Instead of the regular model-stands I like to have a set of boxes that can be arranged in different heights; also some pads so you can have all kinds of lying-down and semi-recumbent poses. A set of steps is good for action poses.

It would be desirable to have two models posing in the class room. One holding an all week pose, the other taking short poses. You can't make much of a drawing in less than ten minutes, but action poses are good to study from. If the model has had some training in dancing you can have short poses that are arranged in sequence to show how the body works in action.

In these action poses look at the model for at least a minute before starting to draw. Draw a diagram of the action. Get the swing of the spine, the muscles that are essential to the position. Perhaps you may not draw at all. Just as well, if you are really comprehending the pose.

Turn the thing into geometric action. Draw it as strongly as you think it. Don't just map the directions of lines, saying, in the case of a twisting pose, "Now, let me see. One leg comes out half way down the arm and the other comes out of the wrist." Draw as though you felt the shapes like a sculptor. Some drawings of the body in contorted positions seem to say, "Isn't it remarkable how little like a human being a human being looks in this position!" *Explain* the three-dimensional structure.

Have The Courage of Your Convictions

Look for a reason to draw when you are making a study. Don't creep up on the drawing as though you were going to poison it. If you can't help yourself, make it bad, but learn something. It is not what you draw that counts, but what you learn, what you add to your subconscious equipment. Any drawing is worthwhile which teaches you something while you are making it; because you observe nature and practise with the graphic tools.

Never mind if it isn't the right form, the shape that you would like to be able to make some day, but make it realized. Make it positive. Define it surely. Then you can see where it is wrong. You can carve into it. If your definition is timid how can you know whether it is good or bad?

Don't get into an easy habit of dashing off smart looking sketches. Drawing is the ability to put down on paper the thing your mind desires to express. It is not putting down the "right" line, for no such thing exists. It is putting down the line of your mental intention. A drawing is a document. It tells what you thought, what you knew and felt about the subject. If a drawing has only one good quality it is worthwhile. The problem is to get a dominant theme of realization all the way through, to establish a critical basis for correcting minor faults.

A good drawing shows that the artist had an easy familiarity with the forms. It has a quiet, serene condition that I call "the art life." After you have that you lose your dependence on the facts in nature. Until you wake up the creative spark, the impulses all come from the subject. Keep your serenity when the full vitality of the picture is nearly reached. Get the excitement and keep the excitement, but let your execution be controlled. The mind finds what the heart feels and calmly dictates it to the hand.

Plan what you are going to say, and then work with no hesitation, as though you had an etching needle in your hand. Don't use the eraser until you have to. Correct a poor line with a more positive one. Don't fuss around timidly.

It takes more knowledge and more vision to keep the livingness in a drawing worked on for three hours than in one made in twenty minutes. One of the things that makes an artist is the ability to work more slowly and still keep the look of impulse. Most good drawings are a combination of speed and advance calculation.

Slow drawings that are worked on by the week become drudgery and look tired and old. Put in the major darks and lights at the same time that you swing in the line structure. Work all over the paper and do not stop to fill in details until you have the whole design established. Keep the lines and tones working together or you will lose unity.

Take a point of view about the subject. Decide what to put in and what to leave out. If you were to put in all the facts you see in nature, even accurately, it wouldn't be worthwhile. It wouldn't be art or truth.

Train yourself to use memory and imagination, or your drawing will show that the model and not your spirit dominated the idea. Memory drawing helps to give one a realization of the Thing. The only trouble with it is that one tends to draw the way someone else did. One loses the impulse from nature and draws with too much formula.

On the other hand it is the figure on your canvas that matters. Your drawing will be judged by it. Remember that, when you are over-worried about likeness. After you have arrived at what you want in one area of the canvas, the model is only there to go back to as a source of stimulation. The canvas is now more important.

Have a special prejudice about the composition of the figure that you can carry through to the completion of the drawing. If it is a neutral pose, decide whether you want it to rise or to spread out.

Pick out some forms that are characteristic of the figure. If the pose builds up in a triangle, look for triangles and pyramids and cones in the figure. Have some plan in seeing the forms.

Leonardo, Ingres, and Delacroix built their forms within ovals and cylinders. They had a plan of beauty which they followed in the selection of lines. Rubens' treatise on drawing says that all forms are contained within squares, triangles, and circles. In your analysis of things it is a matter of personal selection which forms you decide shall be fundamental. Dürer sometimes used cubes or cylinders. He made many interesting experiments in cubism, others on laws of numerical proportion. The Italians were constantly concerned with theories of beauty based on geometrical plans. When a man is a great master this interest in mathematics serves to discipline his thought rather than to devitalize it.

Be sure that you approach the drawing of the figure and the accessories with the same attitude. Keep one tempo all through the drawing. If you get the surroundings too complicated the drawing won't be able to speak, it will stutter. Find some areas in repose, some simple spaces. This doesn't mean to let go of the sense of existence in the background, but let it be a foil for the figure.

Some figures seem to have round tops, you go right over them into space. Realization has something to do with establishing and defining the thing, stopping it and defining the space around it. You have to keep control over the spaces, keep them in touch with the plastic relief you have set up. An air pocket, real space, does not belong in the order of realization of which art is made.

Concern yourself with the body as a thing in action that you understand. The figure should be well-knit. Go after form, not the minor flats and rounds, but the significant planes. Go after continuity, rhythm. Emphasize bones, grooves, posture. Clarify the planes. Get the geometric rhythms of the figure without letting them interfere with the human pulse of the thing. Then find a few muscular moments to chat about. Don't try to put in every muscle. The drawing won't exist. Say one or two human things about the figure that will bring the drawing to life.

If you want to bring a knee forward, do it with a sign: maybe by putting a dark in back of it; perhaps by putting a culminating dark on the front of the knee. Draw it forward. Invent a way to say projection. But you can't make the knee come forward unless the whole figure has bulk and existence to support the plastic corner of the leg.

Find some textural turn to make a culmination in the drawing. Feel something about the vitality of that corner projecting toward you that will make it possible for you to describe it even more strongly on your paper than it exists in nature. Find a texture-symbol to say projection.

Even if you can't see the other arm, you must know what it is doing and you must make us know what it is doing.

Note the plastic texture of the figure. Something that looks as though it were made of steel wool or clock springs mashed together is just an art school technical trick. Get the difference between bone and fat and muscle. Get a dominant fleshy texture to run through the whole drawing of the figure. Don't make the same kind of texture on the drapery and furniture as on the figure.

Don't linoleumize your work. Let the surfaces have vitality, the homely tremor of life. Let some free nebulous tones work under the culminating textural activity. Don't polish it up like a hard-boiled egg. Get some nervousness into the texture surfaces. This doesn't mean to make them haphazard, but get some livingness into them. Live art is what you want to make.

Be a little afraid of using the side of the lithograph crayon too much, for fear of becoming one of the "eggshell" school of drawing, that rounded oval cult which quite mechanically rounds off every object. I prefer to see you make a drawing that is full of corners, kinks.

Get some nerve into the line. When the describing line is always of one width the result is dull and furniture-like. The hands and legs partake of the nature of furniture instead of being human members.

Sometimes the outline looks like the edge of a very good drawing that has been cut out of a piece of paper. And then very stupid sculpturing goes on inside of that line.

You may place the drawing with some light, nebulous lines, but avoid the vagueness of a searching outer edge. Don't look too much for where the leg is going to be, look for what the leg is and what it is doing. Define the edge of it with lines, if you wish. If you are sculpturing with lines or tones that is no excuse for a careless containing line.

An outline drawing must have a sculpturesque point of view. Sometimes, after you have been making a labored, texture-covered drawing, lay a piece of tracing paper over it, and translate it into line. Do not trace the edges but make the drawing over many times until the line concept is complete. Look out for the wiry outline, the cracker-like edge. Make it a life-line, a clumsy, living thing. Look at the work of Daumier. See how his line defines and describes, how it flows—nothing casual about it. Then there is Ingres, master of an exact line that is vital, significant.

When you can make a fairly adequate figure, start digging into the separate parts of the body, making special studies, thorough drawings of them. Make hands and feet as well as the head and torso. Perhaps draw one part of the leg in action, or study a foot that is gripping the floor. Draw the head from underneath or from the top. Be familiar with the forms in all positions.

Sometimes change from line technique to brush and wash; change your tool from the pen to charcoal or lithograph crayon. At other times use paint. Tempera is good to study with because it has a dry, sculptural quality. The advantage of paint is that you can draw light into dark as well as dark on light. This can be done in charcoal by using a kneaded rubber, but not so freely.

Make things and not appearances. Think arm—think of the inside, how it is made. Construct the arm in your mind. Form the idea, arm, in your mind and then play with it. Imagine the arm in different positions. Turn it over in your mind. See it with the elbow flexed, or the fist clenched. Go through all the possible actions of the hand, see what happens to the muscles of the forearm and upper arm. Study your own arm in the mirror. Never mind how many muscles make an action or what their names are, but get a feeling for the mechanics of the action. Have an innate sense of the contraction that has to occur at the elbow when the forearm and hand are pulled up to the shoulder.

After you get the idea, arm, in your mind start to think of different kinds of arms. When you have nothing to do for a few minutes, get in the habit of running through your knowledge of things. Imagine a whole set of arms: bony ones, muscular ones; firm arms, arms that are quiet. Then set them in action.

Have that kind of knowledge of the whole human figure. Be able to play with your general idea of the human body, to modify it at will. Having an idea of the geometric scheme of the human frame, be able to visualize it in different measures. Be able to dress it up with a muscular and fatty tissue make-up that is in keeping with the skeleton you are thinking about.

It is this kind of knowledge that Daumier was referring to when he said, "If you show me an ear I will draw you the head."

The Clothed Figure

A clothed human being has just as much life as a nude. You don't have to make it look as though it were a nude showing through clothes. No muscular information comes through a heavy suit of clothes, only the big masses of the form show. Don't forget that the folds and wrinkles are very small details compared to the big plastic bulk. Subordinate them to the design of the whole figure.

In drawing drapery, notice that the cloth lies flat on the point of contact with the form underneath. You see the shape of the under-form there. The folds run from one point of contact to another, falling free or taut. You must understand the purpose of the fold, how it follows the gesture. Study the system the folds work on, diagram them. Find out how different materials fall and crease, angularly, softly, crisply.

Avoid clever little quirks, dinky folds. Just use those wrinkles which explain the solid action of the figure. Leave some out, and put in others where they will explain the gesture. Try not to let your concern with the folds labor the work.

Make many thorough drawings of the clothed model. Charles Keene's drawings in *Punch* may be studied. Make studies of cloth draped over chairs, and other things. Learn how to draw a dress falling over the bent knee. Notice how you can see the form of the leg along the thigh and calf, how the trouser hangs loose with points of contact.

If you are drawing a foreshortened drapery as over a projecting knee, put more wrinkles near the front. Put the small wrinkles near the front, and larger ones on the far side. It adds to the realization of the bulk by resisting perspective. The same is true of drawing a striped suit. Make the stripes on the near side of the form smaller and closer together and more bitter than those on the far side. Emphasize tangibility on the front corners.

FIGURE DRAWING

Study the model in action poses. Make sketches in restaurants and on the street. Get the character of clothes, the hang of a coat that has been worn.

Draw shoes and gloves, hats, overcoats. Find out how a collar moves around the neck. Make your people belong in the clothes.

Shoes seem to be one of the hardest things for the art student to draw. Or are they too easy? At any rate students are seldom able to draw a shoe so it doesn't look like a magazine advertisement. Draw the sole of the shoe first and then construct the foot or shoe on top of it. A foot is just a modified pyramid set into a cylinder, the ankle. Get the form first, then its character.

Character and Portraiture

The essential reason why one head differs from another is a matter of proportion. That is why we know one friend from another on the street, even from the back.

In drawing, you may get the two-dimensional proportions accurately, but when you work with volumes, some of these change.

It is inconceivable that a great artist should paint a likeness—likeness in the cold, hard sense.

Portraiture has something to do with plastic proportions, a sculptural feeling for the understructure of the head. Something so simple and so deep that the greatest portrait in the world would only come near being a portrait. John Butler Yeats, who painted the best British portraits of the Nineteenth Century, said, "a perfect portrait is an embodied dream of the sitter."

Lots of people think the mystery in a Rembrandt is in his philosophy, that he was a great psychologist. But that isn't it. It is the great realization that makes his things so mysterious.

A good portrait keeps going right on through the neck and shoulders and the way the folds occur on the sleeves. It is a great plastic gesture that passes through the bulk of the figure and the arms and hands, and culminates in the head.

Character is just as much a motive for creating a work of art as it ever was. But it should not be the kind of sentimental, visual realism artists were trying for in the Nineties.

Mild caricature of the face defeats the purpose of caricature itself. Characterization of the moment is nothing. Real character runs all the way from fine caricature to the delicacy and grandeur of a great portrait—from Rowlandson to Rembrandt.

When you look at the sitter, first observe the average human proportions, and then look for modifications peculiar to the individual. Decide whether you want to bring out those characteristics by under-statement or emphasis. When the selection is well made the result is beauty and not just character.

Distortion is sometimes an interesting motive. Exaggeration is another matter. It is falsifying fact, and increasing the importance of fact at the expense of truth. Cheap and offensive.

Try to see the model in a new way when you sit down to draw. I don't mean, to see a new species of animal, but find something fresh to say. Make a drawing with a different flavor. Make some that are ugly, others handsome. Make them healthy, sensitive, powerful. Go deep into the character and find noble proportions in the structure. Use only those details and facts that will contribute to the realization of your concept.

Be kind to people. They wouldn't be alive if they were not fit to live. People are funny enough without our being cruel to them. Some think Daumier was a caricaturist, a satirist, but he was never cruel. His people may look like elephants or earthworms, but exaggerated as they may be they are three times as human as people could ever be. They all belong to the same human family. The same thing is true of Rembrandt's portraits. They are all family portraits, pictures of himself. He was finding himself. If you go deep enough into life you find yourself.

Students find it hard to create on a portrait because they are so concerned with superficial likeness that they are afraid to use their imagination. You must find something that strikes you about the person; put it down as your point of view. Find something that is a dominant plastic gesture: the impulse of the forehead; the "forward to the nose" concept; the set of the eyes in relation to the cheekbones that may show the special character of the individual.

Beauty is not the only thing that inspires the real artist. Some people are so ugly that they are interesting. Take a sculptured portrait by Despiau or Epstein. Every four inches there is an ugliness that no portrait painter would dare put in, but the whole thing is beautiful.

Daumier worked from the skull outward. In his drawings, he searched around until he found the general shape of the head; next he decided what emphasis he wanted to place on the proportions; then he clinched his idea of the person. You don't have to do it that way. You may come to the subject with a preconceived idea of the proportions you are going to use.

Do not make the forehead a mere blend of three or four tones. The fact that they blend keeps it from being a solid. Think of the cubic structure of the form, think of the bones that lie under the skin. Draw the forehead through the temples and join it into the bridge of the nose and the angle of the cheekbones. Draw the big shape of the head and then let the hair grow on it delicately at the edges. The hair doesn't burst out like porcupine bristles.

Look out for magazine-cover hair, slimy, oozing tones with greasy highlights. Make the hair a shape that has weight and texture. Then make it soft with a few well selected comments. They may be a softening of edges at the forehead and around the contour of the head, a few delicate lines here and there.

Never make the shadow under the neck as dark as it looks. The cast shadow painted by most portrait painters looks like a hammock slung under the chin. As for the highlights which are the stock in trade of such "professional painters," the last refuge of an empty mind—I am too much in earnest at this moment to joke about them.

The artist does not see both eyes alike. There is always "the eye" and the other eye. But you shouldn't know that he felt that while he was working. It adds life and plasticity to the drawing if the eye in the light is darker than the one in the shadow. It gives the head vividness. The eyebrow is the last thing. It is just a color and texture accident, happening on the edge of the eyesocket.

Look at the grand design in a Rembrandt portrait. Nothing theatrical about it, nothing grandiose. Just his serving girl standing in the window with one hand resting on the sill and the other on the wall. How grave and rich and human it is. The simple folds of her dress, the hang of the sleeves. The indication of some lace. The texture of hair and flesh and cloth. A bit of ribbon used to describe the neck and shoulders. With what humanity he painted not only that humble human head and hands, but the place. Painted with such understanding that the girl has nobility. Painted and recorded a mental reality no eye could see.

CHAPTER VII

PAINTING

PAINTING IS DRAWING, with the additional means of color. Painting without drawing is just "coloriness," color excitement. To think of color for color's sake is like thinking of sound for sound's sake. Who ever heard of a musician who was passionately fond of B flat? Color is like music. The palette is an instrument that can be orchestrated to build form.

I am interested in the use of colored tones to build solids and as an added means to composition. The great painters separated form and color as a means to realization. They did it by underpainting the form in semi-neutral colors and bringing that sculptured low relief into plastic existence by superimposed color glazes.

A painting may be a thing, the sculpture of the thing, or it may also have color-texture. The painting that has only color has nothing; the painting that has only sculpture has a great deal. A Persian miniature has handsome color, color used to emphasize the design and texture of two-dimensional forms. A Masaccio fresco has little color quality, but tremendous form. A Rembrandt, a Titian, a Rubens, has great form and color-plastic realization.

Drawing is more abstract than painting because line is more abstract than color. It is difficult to retain significant drawing when we use color because we have the means to imitate what we see in nature. We forget to use color as a sign in the same way that we use black and white as a graphic symbol in building form.

Chase used to say, "See it in paint." I beg to differ. He and Sargent belonged to the school that saw nature as active oil paint. But you must learn how to transcribe your graphic thoughts into the medium of color and paint. The craftsmanship of handling paint and the complications of the additional color symbols make a good painting much more difficult to achieve than a good drawing. It takes a great deal of discipline to see your way through the process of building up a picture from the first rough lines to the final result. There are many procedures and formulas, from which you must work out the one best suited to your temperament. There are many things you must know about your pigments and vehicles in order to get the qualities you want, and to make a painting that will be permanent. It is part of a painter's job to know his craft. Whether his own works endure may be of little importance, but he should carry on the tradition of good craftsmanship for others.

There are many kinds of good painting, but one thing is true of them all: it is the power of drawing which makes a painting great. Carpaccio, Bellini, Veronese, Breughel, Rembrandt, Delacroix, and all the others were great painters because they were draughtsmen.

It is a bad idea to have one painter, say Rubens, as your ideal in painting. You become convinced that there is only one way to paint and shut yourself off from learning things from the other masters.

Find your own technique. Form your own color concept of things in nature. I have no rules for fine color to give you. There are some facts about the craft of painting and the use of the palette which may prove helpful to you. The important thing is to keep on drawing when you start to paint. *Never graduate from drawing.*

Form and Color

I think of a good painting as being a colored low relief with no air pockets. First there is the formative under-substance, the shape of the form that the blind man knows through the sense of touch. This is made with the neutral half-tones that carry the sculpture of the form. Clench your fist and bear down on it with the other hand. That solidness, that bulk, must be created on the canvas. It should be sculptured, not modelled. It may be done with two or three tones, or with three hundred.

This under-substance is given realization by super-imposed color textures, force colors. Look at the skin on the hand: not just the color of it but the tactile indications of freckles and veins and wrinkles. See the way the blood flows quickly and slowly. There is the life you must force into your painting with significant color-texture. Use the whole gamut of the palette if you wish. Use it wilfully and consistently.

Hold your hand up to your canvas. If the painting has no more signified substance than the living hand it is only eyesight work and could be done better with color photography.

You can't see the separation of form and color in nature. It is a mental concept. When you are conscious of the principle you will find yourself looking at objects and seeing the form and color in different sequences of thought. Toshi Shimizu, who studied with me, told me that Hokusai, the great Japanese draughtsman, called this "the principle of the Thing and its color Skin." If you have a white egg and paint it red you change the color complexion, but you do not change the form.

I harp on this idea because I believe it to be the root principle of form realization. No doubt it is the main reason for the special vitality of the Renaissance masters. Their color is beautiful not only because it is harmonious, but because it is significant.

Titian, Veronese, and Tintoretto were the first great colorists. Renoir found out that Rubens was right and Rubens found out that Titian was right. They belong to the same tradition.

Ingres was a draughtsman; his paintings have sculpture. Courbet was a painter; he painted with tonality, by massing lights and darks and textures. But Delacroix was a great colorist. He probably knew more about color than any other modern master. He orchestrated his colors as a musician composes a symphony. But Rembrandt was the greatest master of drawing and color-plastic realization.

In El Greco and Chardin the principle of realization is the same. A gray and white low relief of geometrical forms brought to life with top colors.

Most pictures painted within the last seventy-five years were made "directly" with opaque oil paint. In other words, the artist was painting form and color at the same time. Good pictures have been painted in this way, but none of them have the plastic realization that can be obtained when the form and color are painted separately.

Delacroix was one of the few men of the Nineteenth Century who understood the principle of separating form and color. In his *Notebooks* there are constant references to the problem of making a picture realized, the technical problem of making powerful form. Even in his day the tradition of craftsmanship was so lost that he had to learn what he could about technique from the scenery painters. Many of his early pictures have darkened and cracked, but the later ones underpainted in tempera are as fresh as the day they were painted.

Renoir, too, had a long struggle to find the proper technical procedure to express his concept of form. In his later work, he too underpainted the form in black and white, bringing it up to color with glazes.

A few artists in Germany carried on the technical tradition of underpainting form and glazing color. The artist who is interested in his materials can learn a great deal from Max Doerner's *The Materials of the Artist*. In the past ten years a number of men in America have been experimenting along the lines of the old methods and taking advantage of modern scientific discoveries. We are slowly building up a new knowledge of sound craftsmanship, for both easel and mural painter.

PAINTING

Having painted for thirty years almost entirely in the direct method, and becoming more conscious of the plastic character of form and the fact that color was a separate quality, I tried to make the separation in my painting not only a matter of thought, but of technical process.

Working in solid oil paint, I started the painting in a general tone that defined the sculpture of the forms. Then I worked up the form and color with stronger statements of value and color. But I was unable to get the real separation of form and color because the opaque paint of the later stages of the painting blended and covered up entirely the sculpture of the thing which had been painted in first. The thought was there but the technical process was inadequate. So it was a conscious desire to paint form and color separately that led me to the procedure of underpainting and glazing. I learned a great deal from Renoir's later work at this time. It was through an analysis of his work that I became conscious of the same principle in the work of the old masters.

My first departures from direct painting were rough impasto underpaintings made with white lead, glazed with oil-varnish medium. The forms were built up in pale semi-neutrals and hues. I let this oil underpainting dry for two days and then glazed it with transparent colors, working quite quickly and not fussing the glazes. It was my hope that the glazes would dry with the top paint skin of the impasto and not cause any cracking. Ten years later no cracking has occurred.

Learning about the advantages of a tempera underpainting which would dry overnight and not darken as oil paint does, I started to use it, At first I had much trouble to find the right medium. I found zinc white was unsatisfactory as a pigment. Later, using a casein emulsion and lead or titanium white, I have been able to work freely without any fear of cracking. I feel pretty certain that all the heavy, staccato impasto paint in the old masters work is made with tempera. Certainly the brilliance of

Flemish and Venetian pictures is the result of the underpainting in tempera which glows through the layers of colored varnish glazes.

A picture which is underpainted with tempera seems to have a light of its own. Like a stained glass window, the light is reflected back from the white ground through the vitreous color glazes. The forms retain their bulk even in candlelight. When you look at a direct painting in a dull light it seems to have no form at all.

Rembrandt's "Jewish Bride" has all the great qualities. It has great plastic realization because the form and color were painted separately. First it was painted as a low relief, built up as a piece of sculpture, with pale tones of gray, naples yellow, and vermillion. The textures of the materials, the flesh, the hair, the background, were loaded up in the lights, drawn with paint. Then some broad washes of color-texture that describe the colors of the things with more force. Greater emphasis on the light and shade to carry the design. These glazes reinforce the sculpture of the thing. On top of these are more tones that bring the form and color into greater realization. Then the culminating tones, the full darks and top textures. There is no imitation of the shadows in nature, no imitation of the colors in nature. The form is made more significant with color-texture. It is more real than the things looked, it is more real than the things could ever be in nature.

Texture is what vitalizes the form. The great painters use color to amplify the sculptural texture of things. Sculptural texture may be achieved by defining the thing with minute details as in a Mantegna or Cranach. It may be done more freely as in a Rubens. He was a master of painting materials, the surfaces of things hard or soft, dull or shiny. But a greater master was Rembrandt. More than any other he used realizing, essential textures, to make the form plastic. He did not use every detail but described the nature of the thing with symbols. There is the dry realization of a Breughel and then there is the signified texture of a Daumier. One

COLOR-TEXTURAL PROGRESSION

Underpainting of form
terre verte and white lead

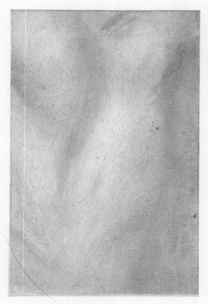

Plus scumbles—
raw sienna and cadmium red

Plus glazes—
alizarine crimson, burnt sienna, Y 5

Plus glazes and linework—
Y3 and raw sienna

See pages 119-123 for explanation of color notations;
pages 136-143 and 175-177 for description of underpainting and glazing.

THE COLOR TRIANGLE

This color diagram represents colors in pigment mixture. Yellow, red, and blue at the points of the equilateral triangle are primary colors. Colors mixed between these points on the outside triangle are secondary colors. All tones within the triangle are tertiary colors. The larger inside triangle runs through the semi-neutral colors. The smallest triangle indicates the hues (very neutral colors.) See page 119 for complete description.

has sculpture, the other has also color-textural description.

We should be able to paint textures at will, not fumble around with paint trying to imitate the way a thing looks. An artist in the old days knew how to use paint to describe things: metal, wood, stone. He knew how to make water, smoke, fire; how to paint bone and muscle and flesh and hair.

A fine painter can paint the quality of light as a thing. Sunlight, daylight, twilight, moonlight, any kind of light; fog and rain; the lights of city streets and interiors. The sense of light can contribute to the realization of the forms and the character of the place.

We have no tradition of painting today. The old masters had methods and formulas. A student was apprenticed from seven to fourteen years to learn his craft. It meant that there was less chance for individual expression, but the work of minor men had infinitely more power than most of our best talents can achieve today. We have been so wrapped up in personal expression that we have lost the power of disciplined technique.

The old masters had definite formulas for making forms and textures. They had color systems. For instance, Rubens had certain color themes which he repeated constantly because they worked in building form and making satisfactory compositions. He used to keep his colors mixed up in jars, well-regulated intervals of darks, half-tones, and lights in each color scale. If he had an order for a mural he could turn the sketch over to his assistants with some notes about using the usual sets of tones for blond flesh color, dark flesh color, green drape, gray horse, and so forth. When everything had been laid in by the assistants he would come along and finish it with a few drawing marks and culminating color tones.

The important thing about those color systems is that they were used as a means to realization. Those men knew that certain sets of tones laid together would make solid form. Once knowing that a chord of color tones would make form, they could transpose it at will to any section of the palette. A knowledge of these means of realization was part of their equipment.*

Cézanne used to say that one should have forty-eight tones set on the palette all the time. He found a set of color-tone intervals that would make form for him. Lots of people are imitating his way, using little Cézanne-isms. Renoir had his way. Titian and Rembrandt had their ways of doing it, and they are so inscrutable that one can scarcely find the formula. But in each case the system is there.

In all fine painting there is an understructure of semi-neutrals and hues: the skeleton of the color composition that carries the form. The full colors are the final skin.

In a picture that is underpainted and glazed you can see the monochromatic form painting that lies underneath the color. More important than the beauty of full color glazes are the optical grays, the half-tones made when the color glaze lies on top of the pale neutral tones that sculpture the form in the underpainting. If the form has been laid in with gray and white everywhere, these gray tones come through the local color glazes and keep the form statement a thing apart.

More color power may be obtained if each form is underpainted with pale tints of the local color, the root hues of the color scale. Still more color power and variety may be had by underpainting a color with tones in an adjacent color scale. Flesh is often underpainted with terre verte which has more color force under a glaze of raw sienna than has a black and white gray. The more you open up the colors in the underpainting, the more control you have to use to keep the painting a harmonious unit.

In direct painting, the color harmony is best planned **on the**

---

*Thirty years ago under the direction of Charles A. Winter, experimenting led Robert Henri, George Bellows, Randall Davey and myself to the use of an arsenal of forty-eight tones, each in three shades, and all in separate stock jars. From these we could rapidly select a particular palette. We used this extension of Maratta's colors for several years. See page 122.

palette. Every stroke of paint laid on the canvas should be right in color, degree of neutrality, and lightness, or it will not stay in key with the rest of the work. When glazing over an underpainting you are free to change the color without re-drawing all the time, as you have to do when painting directly.

Color Powers

I think it is very important for the artist to have a working knowledge of the use of the palette. The palette is an instrument, like a piano or violin. In the hands of a master it may be a complete orchestra. To stumble around in full colors and raw white is as stupid as it would be if a musician were to play the piano wearing boxing gloves.

The most obvious use of color is to give variety to a two-dimensional design worked out in black and white pattern. If the gray tones are translated into two or three colors, the eye moves from area to area of red or green, just as it follows light and dark tones. Likewise a drawing in black chalk on gray paper may be given more variety of color-texture if brown is used to describe different materials or to accentuate the design. Daumier and Toulouse-Lautrec used color in this way when drawing. The spotting of colors in different areas of the design is a decorative device, and while essential to color composition, it is not the most important thing about the use of color.

A significant factor in color is the quality of projection and recession which colors have when laid together. If you look at the spectrum, the hot brilliant oranges and yellows advance toward the eye, while the cool greens, blues, and violets recede. Colors of full intensity advance more than neutral hues. The artist makes use of this dynamic, architectural power of color to build form. By relating one tone to another, he can force the projection and recession of planes in addition to the drawing of form made with black and white symbols.

Color changes alone do not make form. The sculpture of the form is made by significant tones in the black and white scale, the light and shade definition of the thing. Without changes of value, changes of color alone will not make form.

If you were painting a lemon you could make the form move around if it were full yellow at the most projecting point, with sequences to yellow-green and green or yellow-orange and orange—provided that within those color changes there were tone changes to signify the sculpture of the thing. You might paint a lemon with a set of tones in the yellow-purple scale. The moves toward purple would carry the form back.

The most projecting point on the spectrum is yellow-orange; the most receding, blue-purple. Pure yellow has a tendency to turn into light.

Yellow-orange, orange, red-orange, and red seem to be the most tangible colors. This is partly because the eye favors yellow, it sees things easier in yellowish light. Purple is the least tangible color; and many people are not sensitive to the color, cannot see it. Yellow is also a color of intangibility.

Think of a pure color as having the power of black. Some of our pigments are stronger than others, as yellow is lighter in value than red, but if we had such a thing as pure strength colors, they would all look black in the tube. Each color has its own character, weight, insisting quality.

Color tones have to be balanced against each other. A change in the black and white scale or a move toward neutrality, or a shift in color may change the weight of a color, change its place on the form.

The important colors to know about are the neutral, indescribable tones so loosely called grays and browns. These are the tones that set off the projecting, positive colors; these are the tones that construct the form. It is useful to have some system in naming these tones and a knowledge of their composition.

PAINTING

The Color Triangle

I have found the Dudeen color triangle introduced by Charles A. Winter, a very practical color diagram. The triangle represents color mixtures in pigment form more accurately than does the circle. At the three points of an equilateral triangle are the primary colors, red, yellow, and blue. From these are mixed the secondary colors, orange, green, and purple. In pigment mixture, the secondaries are less intense in color than the primaries and consequently closer to the point of neutrality, or center of the triangle. All colors within the outside edge of the triangle are tertiaries.

The triangular diagram shows the full intensity colors around the outside edge, drawn down to the point of neutrality by admixture with the complementary colors of each color scale. Tints with white might be shown by imagining a series of triangles built up above, each section containing more and more white until the top layer is composed of the palest tints. Above this series of triangular diagrams lies white; below it lies black.

White pigment slightly neutralizes any color it is mixed with. Black is not a color, and black pigment deadens any color neutralized by it.

The complementary to a color is its opposite on the triangular diagram, a color which contains none of the other's factors. Purple, made of red and blue contains no yellow, and is that color's complement, and so forth. Notice in the triangular diagram of color that yellow-green is not the complement of red-purple as inaccurately indicated by circular diagrams. In pigment mixture the complement of yellow-green is about two parts red-purple, one part purple. The distance between a secondary color and the point of neutrality is half that of the primary color (its complement) and the point of neutrality. These limitations of the color scales in pigment mixture make the triangle a more practical diagram than the circle for the artist's purposes.

[119]

In order to distinguish between colors of the same color scale at different degrees of intensity, we refer to them as color, semi-neutral and hue. If you mix yellow-green and yellow-orange, you get yellow semi-neutral. If you mix green and orange you get yellow

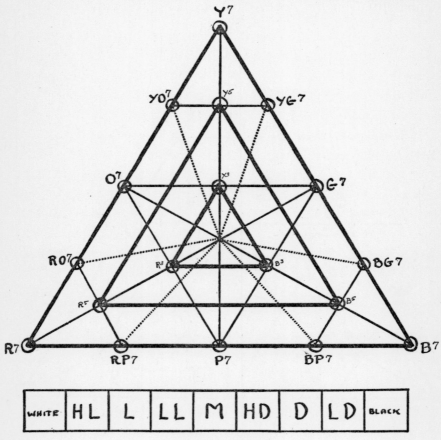

Color Diagram

hue. Thus we have two interior triangles, the semi-neutrals and the hues.

For brief color notations we may call full color Y7, semi-neutral, Y5, hue Y3, etc. This gives one an accurate and simple way of making color notes on sketches.

PAINTING

To describe the degree of white in a tone a scale of heights is useful. High light, light, low light, middle, high dark, dark, low dark. Abbreviated: HL, L, LL, M, HD, D, LD.

The ability to recognize that vermillion, light red, and burnt sienna are all in the same color scale is of the same use to the

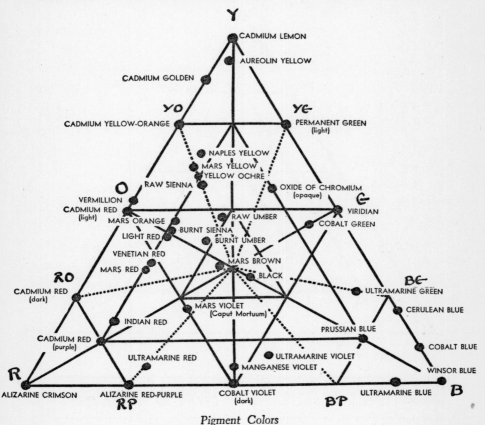

Pigment Colors

artist as the musician's ability to recognize C sharp in one octave and another. The artist should think of orange and blue, red and green, and so forth, as two ends of the same color.

It is good to keep a color diagram up on the wall.* Think about

---

*When you make your own, mix all the tones with a little white so that you can see the color in the semi-neutrals and hues.

color diagrammatically. Know that blue hue can be made by mixing blue with orange or green with purple. Think of blue and its related colors, blue-green and blue-purple, as well as blue, an isolated color moving to orange.

A color-tone has three factors, which may be changed: color scale; degree of intensity (or neutrality) ; and quantity of white.

True yellow is a relatively greenish color, like a lemon cadmium. Alizarine crimson is a true red, which makes a perfect red-green scale with viridian. Orange is not the color of the fruit but a color corresponding to vermillion or cadmium red light. A pure blue lies between ultramarine and cobalt. The new Winsor Blue is a fine, powerful pigment, neither too green nor too purple. Purple has to be mixed by eye. You can test it by pulling down lemon cadmium until you get accurate semi-neutral yellows.

When Hardesty Maratta made his colors I used to get his sets containing complete semi-neutrals and hues accurately mixed. His paints were carefully mixed from the primary colors so that some element of yellow, red, and blue was carried through all the tertiary colors. Since yellow in mixture has a tendency to lighten colors, the hues were lighter and less powerful than those you can make with the earth colors.

Home-made hues can be made as follows: Red hue *equals* Indian red *plus* viridian. Blue hue *equals* ultramarine *plus* burnt umber. Yellow hue *equals* raw umber *plus* a little cadmium yellow.

Useful semi-neutrals to keep on the palette, as well as the earth colors, are: Green *equals* opaque oxide of chromium *plus* ultramarine; purple *equals* caput mortuum *plus* ultramarine; yellow *equals* raw sienna *plus* a little opaque oxide of chromium pulled up by cadmium yellow. Indian red *plus* a little viridian is a good semi-neutral red. Light red or burnt sienna may be used for semi-neutral orange. Ultramarine and light red pulled into the true blue scale by a little green make a good semi-neutral blue.

When making hues and semi-neutrals, test them out with white as it is hard to see what colors they are when full darks. Hues are most useful on the palette when mixed with some white.

Some artists who grind their own colors mix up these color intervals in tubes so they can be renewed on the palette without constant mixing. It is a good idea to keep the palette fully equipped with semi-neutrals and hues all the time. It keeps one from dipping into raw color. It is also more economical because these

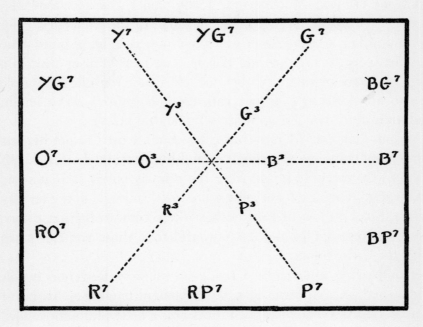

Arrangement of Palette

colors are made almost entirely of the inexpensive earth colors, which are also the most permanent pigments we have.*

I like to use a large table palette that has plenty of room for mixed tones. Metal is preferable because of its neutral color and because old paint can be burned off. Some artists prefer white glass. A large enamel baking tray makes a good palette. It can be

*The Mars colors are artificial earth colors and very powerful, permanent pigments.

filled with water (which keeps the colors from forming skins), if you want to save tones for later work. A good, light hand-palette can be made of common corrugated cardboard covered with parchment paper.

Colors should be laid out on the palette in an orderly way. I prefer to put the full intensity colors around the outside edge of a large rectangular palette. Starting with yellow-orange in the upper left hand corner and moving to yellow and yellow-green around to the right, so that orange and blue come opposite each other at the middle of either side. The neutral tones are then laid along the lines of their color scales. The spaces in between are used for mixtures with white.

Color Composition

One or more colors may be held as dominants. The dominant color may occur in a focused, intense culminating area as an accent of positive color. Or it may be a pervading tonality, a color that modifies all the other colors on the canvas. Thus you may use green as a precious color, a jewel-like note, by setting it among some fine neutrals. Or you may paint a picture with a great variety of greens set off by some tones that are held very simply.

I once mixed up seven or eight completely different greens which, when put on the canvas, all looked the same. This was because I had changed all the surrounding tones so there was no constant foil for them to work against.

Colors are very sensitive to the power of harmony and contrast. While you are working, all the tones are influencing each other. When you put a strong red next to a more neutral color it will bring out red in that tone, if possible. If not, the neutral color will look more green than it really is, because of simultaneous contrast.

The effect of a color is entirely relative. A neutral orange may look green or yellow when laid among some blue-purple notes. A neutral green may look blue when laid beside yellow-greens. This is particularly true of neutral colors, which seem to have little color unless laid together with definite intervals of value and intensity.

Two colors of equal strength tend to arrest each other. When of equal intensity and value, they fight to dominate each other √ and disturb the eye. Thus a contrast of blue and red-orange is more effective than blue and orange because the complementaries are opposite, static.

Two colors juxtaposed or superimposed will make a third color appear. The more complicated the color scheme the more difficult it is to control the influence of one color on another.

The simplest use of color in painting that is concerned with solid forms is definition of each thing with a positive local color. The early Italians and Flemish used it in this way to reinforce the pattern of the design. When the form and color are separated, the local colors may be held positively, or they may be subordinated to the light and shade design. In a Rembrandt, a black velvet sleeve may be struck with light or a white collar be drawn with dark tones to keep the forms related to the design. Likewise with color: a red hat may be drawn in the shadow with neutral purple and dark yellow-orange while coming up to full crimson in the light, if these are colors that help to bind the design together. Color tones help to weave the separate forms into a unified concept. Whether you wish to emphasize the form of each thing as a unit, or the design of the thing as a whole, you must decide which direction the work is to take and stick to it.

A painting with strong, color-textural realization is kept under control by foils of simply held color areas. A foil may be a neutral color or a positive one, a half-tone, light or dark, depending on the requirements of the design.

Rembrandt often used masses of light and dark as foils. In color he generally would hold some area, say a cool neutral half-tone, as a foil for the palpitating color changes of the other surfaces.

Rubens used big areas of full intensity local color (oranges, reds, blues, greens, and several positive neutral half-tones) as foils to bring out the color in the flesh. Flesh tones that appear to be strong oranges, greens, and rose are made with earth colors, and grays scumbled with yellows. They are laid side by side, with strong intervals in the black and white scale and alternations of warm and cool tones. The color in those semi-neutrals is brought out by the surrounding colors. The colors in a Rubens don't vibrate. Each tone is a positive sculpturing color-texture that takes its place on the form.

In a Renoir, the flesh generally is held as a simple color area surrounded by a background of palpitating color-changes. The colors are so subtly woven in and out that the eye can pick up yellow and read it all through the design, then green, and so forth. His paintings are almost always dominated by a culminating red color-texture.

All of Titian's and Rembrandt's pictures were painted in the orange scale with exceptions—that is, painted in the orange scale with other color notes used as accents.

Delacroix was a great innovator in the use of color. He broke away from the hide-bound system of working in tones of the earth colors and opened up the whole palette. He learned things from Constable and was stirred to the use of full colors by his trip to Algeria; but perhaps the most important things he learned about color came from a study of Chevreul, the great color theorist. Chevreul demonstrated many of the optical properties of color, color recession, simultaneous contrast and its influence on color harmony, and so forth. Delacroix experimented with these ideas and used them to increase the power of color in realizing form. He worked out his compositions in color on the palette. He used color system but was never dominated by any one formula. Each picture was painted with a specially designed palette set with key notes, colors of specific composition as to intensity and height. He could then draw with paint, vividly and subtly.

Form and Local Color

The color of the thing, the local color, is at its fullest intensity in the light. The color in the shadow is more neutral. If the material is opaque with no surface color-texture, the shadow is a neutral of the same color scale. The reflected light appears brilliant in contrast to the shadow, but is not as high in color intensity as the color in the full light. The reflected light is affected by the color of the surface which is reflecting the light. Full, strong sunlight somewhat neutralizes colors containing no yellow. These are facts which the painter may use, or change at will.

When you analyze the local color of a thing in nature, walk around and study it both in the light and shade. Think of the form and color separately, and decide what neutral is the sculpturing tone of the shadows that lies under a skin of color, the complexion. It may be raw umber and white, terre verte and white, or black and white that you see lying under raw sienna to make a certain color of flesh. Even if you are going to paint directly try to think of the neutral sculpturing tones in the shade and light.

The fundamental color recession formula for building form is a series of intervals from a light note of high intensity color moving to darker notes of more neutral tones in the same scale. A variation of this would be to move from orange to yellow hue instead of from orange to orange hue.

Another symbol is the alternation of warm and cool color-tone intervals. When combined with changes in the scale of heights and intensity of the colors, this is a very powerful symbol. For example: yellow semi-neutral light, yellow-orange semi-neutral low light, yellow hue middle, yellow-green semi-neutral low light, and so forth.

The symbol of warm and cool recession which is most neglected is the one which is inherent in the spectrum itself: the fact that red-orange looks cool next to orange, recedes from orange; yellow-green projects more than green; green more than blue-green. By using this symbol for warm and cool, projection and recession, you can make a color cooler, more receding, without making it more neutral.

It is very important to bear in mind this principle about the spacial recession of colors. If you are painting a street at night, make the lights in the foreground yellow-orange, running in a sequence back to red-orange in the background, with similar changes in the colors of the buildings. If you were to put a strong yellow-orange on a plane in the background that is made with neutral purples, it might jump out of place. Orange would look like yellow-orange with those tones and stay in place.

The student should spend a great deal of time mixing tones on the palette to learn their composition. Studies should be made of the simple solids. At first use the monochromatic symbol, tones in one color scale. Then practise with the other color symbols, working out your own means for building form. Sometimes work with tones in the limited inner triangle of hues. Find out what the colors are and what they will do for you.

Color Harmony and the Use of Set Palettes

The twelve major color divisions of the triangle, yellow, yellow-green, green, etc., may be compared to the twelve half-tones of the musical scale. Chords of color-notes based on well-established numerical harmonies may be used for the dominant colors of a composition. Groups of colors selected from the twelve notes of the spectrum arranged in intervals of 3-4-5, etc. have inherent harmony.

Most systems of color harmony have been based on the combination of complementaries. Such combinations are static because the complementaries are opposites that equalize each other. The use of triad chords based on thirds, fifths, and sevenths as in music, brings out the dynamics.

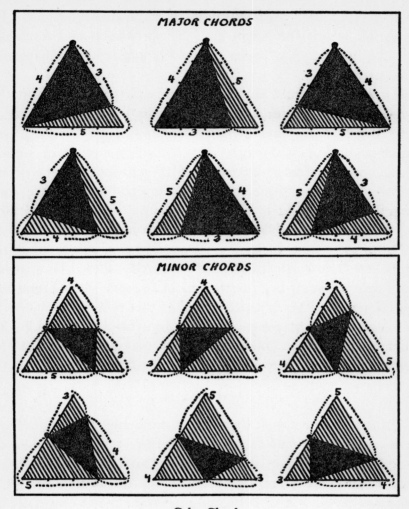

Color Chords

A palette limited by a triad, such as red, yellow-orange, and blue-green retains the elements of the twelve color scales. The dominant colors are emphasized by omitting other full colors from the palette—those other colors being represented by notes of lower intensity. A minor chord contains no full primary color.

For instance, in a palette limited to the triad of purple, yellow-orange, and green, when you draw lines on the triangle between those points you cut off all the positive blues, blue-greens, and blue-purples. The top corner of positive yellow and yellow-green is omitted. The whole section of reds and oranges is cut off. But you still have a relative blue in blue hue, a relative yellow in yellow semi-neutral, and a relative red in a low red hue. With this controlled palette you have a means that is less imitative than the full gamut of colors.

✓ In selecting colors for a picture I do not choose them at random. If I like the color of an orange smock and feel that a background of yellow wall would not contribute to that orange, I may shift the yellow note to yellow-green. In choosing another important color for my palette (using a 3-4-5 triad), I may decide arbitrarily on blue-purple or purple—whether I see that color in nature or not —because it would be harmonious and useful with those other colors.

✓ I lay these notes on my palette, and make some in-between mixtures that lie along the lines of the triangle of which orange, yellow-green, and blue-purple are the outside points; also semi-neutrals and hues which lie in that color range.

✓ Then I make further decisions, establishing a scale of heights. Perhaps the orange is to be middle height, full color; the yellow-green to be light, and slightly modified by some blue-purple; the blue-purple to be low dark, containing no white at all. Then I mix up some tones for other areas of the canvas, hues and semi-neutrals that are related to the dominant colors, and well separated in color and height interval so they will hold as positive notes against each other. I select these tones to bring out the color character of the dominant colors, to act as foils. I now have a tone on the palette for each area of local color.

For modifying tones, tones to mix with the general color of each area, to sculpture with, I now mix a set of lights, darks, and half-tones that are varied in color and intensity. Perhaps, three tones to lighten with: a cool one of white with a little blue-green semi-neutral; a warm white containing a little raw sienna; and a neutral white. Then medium lights, darks and so forth. Bearing in mind the need to modify that orange smock with a yellowish tone, a greenish or reddish tone, I now can say what I want about it.

With these set tones, I paint as though I were using colored chalks, not dipping in raw white or raw color. All modifications are made by mixing these notes together for sculpturing gradations or texturings.

After working for a while, I may decide to extend the orange note to yellow-orange and red-orange to increase the color-range. I mix up more tones on the palette that will be related to the set scale of heights already established.

With a very limited palette it is hard to do much color trilling, use of color recessions. Now that I have a range of color from yellow-orange to red-orange, I can use those colors to force the projection and recession of the form more powerfully than I could with the tones made up to sculpture. If I mix a little yellow-orange with the orange to paint a projecting form, and mix some red-orange with the orange to paint a receding form, the general color will still look orange, but those color changes are acting as strong signs to make the form move back and forth.

Such modifications may be so subtle that the eye doesn't know they are there, but they have great significance. The principle can be used in painting the round cylinder of an arm, in changing the color of stripes on a drapery, or in the painting of two forms of the same color in different planes. If you are painting a still life of some red apples, make those in the foreground move toward orange, those in the background move toward red-purple. This saves your changes toward the more neutral tones for sculpturing each individual form. I do not mean that you should always do this. It is a perfectly good sign to paint a house in the foreground with vermillion and one in the background with venetian red.

An infinite number of color combinations may be worked out by practising with set palettes. It is something I advocate as a means of control rather than a method of obtaining richly orchestrated color. It is a means of discovering new color relations when you get too much in the habit of using one formula. Even the artist who is underpainting and glazing can learn things by making sketches and studies with set palettes arranged for direct painting.

If you organize your palette from nature you get a greater variety of color sequence than if you limit yourself to a preconceived logical scheme. If you are painting from memory, make color notes on your drawings that will help you set your palette. Analyze the color of a thing into the fundamental root tone, the sculpturing tone, and the color-texture. If a street looks greenish underneath a surface of dirty orange you may put down some specific remarks: G3-M under YO2-HD. When you paint your picture, you may decide to transpose those tones into another color scale, but you have some notes about the relative color qualities that will help you.

If you use the same kind of color tone to dig a hole in one place and to make form in another, they will fight to say the same thing. If the greenishness of the flesh is too close in color and value to a green area in the background the tones on the flesh will make holes through to the plane of the background.

When part of an area is cut off by a surrounding form, as a piece of background seen through a bent arm—let that cut-off area partake somewhat of the surrounding form in color and tone. If the background is a dark blue, lighten the area and move the color more toward the warm side of the palette. Otherwise the simultaneous contrast of values and colors will break up the plane of the front form.

Where the edge of one color comes against another, don't just smudge the paint together. Decide whether you want to emphasize the edge with greater color contrast, or to relax the form by making a move toward a common color.

Keep the separate color areas of the design related to each other. Use semi-neutrals and hues that partake of the color-nature of different positive color areas. This is sometimes called painting one thing into another, putting some color from the neighboring form into an area whether you see it there or not. Harmony is based on the principle A:B as B:C. The common factor makes for harmony of tone and color.

Light and Color

The sun is our source of white light, which is made up of all the colored rays of the spectrum. A pigmented surface absorbs certain rays of light and reflects others. Thus a green leaf absorbs red rays and reflects green rays.

It is well to remember that a beam of light cannot be seen unless the atmosphere is charged with dust, smoke, fog, or other suspended particles.

Direct sunlight has a neutralizing effect on color. The most intense color generally is seen in the reflected light; that is why grass often looks greener in the shade.

In north light, the artist's working light, the color of the form is most intense in the lightest areas. When the light is subdued, as in twilight, oranges and reds darken faster than greens, blues, and purples. A blue dress, the same value as a red dress, will look lighter and higher in key than the red one.

Moonlight is just sunlight reflected from a button in space, the moon. I painted a moonlight landscape once. I took eight tones from black with a little white in it to white with a little black in it. Then I mixed a tone for the local color of each thing, as seen in daylight. I painted the picture in daylight, modifying the colors of the things with those eight black and white tones. It is knowing how much white you want in each tone that counts. The picture has real moonlight. It is mysterious and moonlight is mysterious.

In painting night-lighted subjects, it is very difficult to carry the color of the light through the picture; to carry not only the tonal quality but also the color character. It may be done by mixing all the lights with a colored white.

If you see two objects, one red and one green, under a red light, the red object will look white and the green object will look black. The red-colored pigment reflects all the light and the green-colored pigment absorbs all the light.

If you are painting something under artificial yellow-orange light, first mix tones for the local colors as they are in daylight. Then make a set of tones from white with a little yellow-orange in it to yellow-orange with a little white in it. Use the set white with the least color in it to modify the lightest things, such as white tablecloths. Use the set tone with the least white to modify the dark colors. A set of semi-neutral and neutral tones in the yellow-orange scale may be used to modify the color of the forms in the shadow. This principle is true for artificial lights of any color.

Drawing for Painting

I like to see students, especially those who are thinking of painting, make drawings with texture all over in the light, drawings that look like bronze; drawings in which the form is defined completely. Drawings that are fully realized are the best kind of material to paint from. They may be done with wash and pencil, or charcoal, or pen and ink linework.

There is a better chance of getting an exciting painting from a labored study with texture than from a fine drawing without it. One finds oneself trying to imitate the drawing symbols of the latter rather than inventing a way to say it with tones in paint.

It is always wise to make a black and white sketch before painting. It helps you to keep your mind on the design and structure of the forms, and to avoid being carried away by color niceties.

Say that you have a drawing to work from. You could mix up a general tone for the white of the paper, different in each area of local color. Then other sets of tones for the grays and near blacks. Then some tones to work on these the way pen lines and granular markings work over the washes and smudged tones of the drawing. You may use lines to say lines, or translate the drawing into tones and textures.

It would be interesting to take a Rembrandt drawing and translate it into color. You might lay in the broad tones with neutrals and semi-neutrals, and then drive into it with colored lines. Use color sequence in the linework. It helps to turn things, makes formal changes more comprehensible.

Get a set of colored pencils or crayons, one that has good neutrals and semi-neutrals. Make colored drawings with them, using combinations of two to five or six colors at a time. Make the form with a low key color and then put in the top textures with a fuller-intensity color. You can put in the color-textures with linework, so the lines act as glazes over the under-form. See the difference between a tone that lies all over the surface of the white paper, and one made of lines between which the light of the paper shines through. If you use a number of pencils, well separated in color, you can get strong color sequences. Such drawings are good material to paint from.

Also make drawings with water color, using changes in color to signify changes of plane and color-texture. Water color is best used as a drawing medium, combined with pencil or penwork.

A painting should not look like a colored drawing. The thing that looks like a tinted drawing is a minor kind of painting. But one of the things we are apt to lose in our painting is the quality that a drawing has, because the white paper surface keeps on going under the washes and granular tones. The continuous surface of the form under the color is hard to retain when we are painting.

Underpainting and Glazing

The principle of underpainting and glazing is the separation of form and color. The form is painted in opaque monochromatic tones very pale in key. On top of this sculptured low relief, transparent and translucent colors are laid or rubbed in films, like water color washes. This is called glazing. Because light is reflected through the films of color they are more luminous and intense in color than if the same tone were imitated by mixing white with the same color. Thus the gamut of color power is greater in glazed painting than in direct painting.

The underpainting may be made of pigments ground in oil or varnish, but it is preferable to use tempera emulsion. Tempera dries completely in a few hours and does not darken with age the way oil does.*

The glazes are applied with an oil varnish medium. The paint surface stays wet enough to be worked on for about twelve hours and is dry in twenty-four. The glazes eventually dry to a tough durable film that cannot be removed without turpentine and a stiff brush.

The underpainting should be a positively sculptured low relief. I like to have the lights thick—but not too thickly painted, to give some "bite" to the glazes and to get a sense of texture in the light. Only by experience can you learn how dark in value the tones should be. Generally speaking what we call "pastel" is dark enough.

The underpainting should be neutral and preferably cool in color. Positive colors may be underpainted with shaded tints of the full color. This is especially true of blues and reds because the oil glazes darken or fade. Reds are best underpainted with vermillion or cadmium. Greens with yellow, and so forth. The colored undertone supports and gives luminosity to the glazes.

---

*See Chapter X, Notes on Painting Technique, page 166. Tempera painting requires considerable experience with the medium.

Many of the old pictures were underpainted with a black and white gray. This has a tendency to deaden the colors. Blue hue has more life. Terre verte is the most useful color for underpainting flesh. Sometimes I have used raw umber for figures in artificial light; or a tint of cadmium red when I wanted to get the rosy feeling under a golden skin.

Rubens and Rembrandt often used black, naples yellow, and red ochre. Veronese underpainted with a great deal of full color, which is one reason his things have retained their freshness. Sometimes the underpainting was made on a toned ground of gray, terre verte, or Indian red. The forms were built up with white or white and gray. If the toned ground is washed thinly over the gesso it does not detract from the luminosity of the picture. Unfortunately, many artists used dark red grounds which have come through the top painting, darkening the whites and changing the color.

There is reason to think that the old masters used a great deal of system in planning the underpainting colors. Instead of using a neutral of the local color glaze they would underpaint with a hue of an adjacent color scale: as flesh is often underpainted with terre verte, a semi-neutral yellow-green three notes away from the yellow-orange of flesh color. To carry this out systematically, one would underpaint a red-purple with a low orange or low blue, and so forth.

The underpainting does not have to be monochromatic in each area. One might use blue hue for the dark, purple semi-neutral for the half-tone and red-orange color for the light. A controlled use of color intervals in the underpainting simplifies the glazing a great deal.

Avoid putting dark neutrals in the underpainting. They are impossible to paint out if you want to change them to colored darks in the subsequent painting.

When the underpainting is dry (and "isolated" in the case of tempera), you are ready to glaze. Use a sable brush and wash on the colors as you would water color. Work in the glaze with the brush, rag, and fingers until it is smooth. Part of it may be removed with a rag. If the underpainting is rough the color may be lifted off the surface of the lights by dragging the rag across the impasto. When the glaze is freshly applied it may be completely removed by an absorbent rag. When it has set you have to use turpentine. If the underpainting is made with oil, you must be careful not to dissolve it with the turpentine.

The first glaze should carry the gist of the local color in a fairly light key but of not too neutral intensity. I almost always have some white in the first glaze because it works well on top of the opaque underpainting. This scumble brings out fine optical grays as it lies over the under-tones. Then I modify this general color statement with some color-textural changes that do not alter the tone very much. I work them in with the thumb until I get a dry-looking, palpable surface. After this I reinforce the cool, neutral tones of the underpainting with similar tones higher in key. *It is very important not to paint out the underpainting which carries the form.* Don't lose the cool tones that come through in the light to define the form.

At this stage I let, or I ought to let, the painting dry overnight. Then I decide on some positive color-textures, and try them out all over the picture. You can't tell whether a color is going to work unless you carry it out to some conclusion. Other colors are affected, new relations are set up. I try to work with some system: first going through with warm tones and then with cool ones; carrying yellow notes through the design, green notes, blue, and so forth—weaving the thing together and forcing color intervals to work in building the forms. If these tentative notes work together I leave them as textures and drawing marks, or else rub them into the under-glazes to make tonal gradations. If they are not right they can be wiped off the dry glazes underneath.

When an area gets muddy, or the underpainting has been

choked by too much scumbling, clean off all the glazes down to the underpainting. Build up the glazes as you did in the beginning. Do not think you can imitate a tone made of three or four glazes and scumbles, with a single wash.

Always think of drawing, getting the forms realized, emphasizing the design.

If you are working from the model be careful not to imitate what you see in color-texture—get beyond that.

At this point it is sometimes good to build up the forms with white, to improve the drawing, renew the luminosity of the lights, and put in details. Thick scumbles of white may be laid over "dead" areas and drawn into with impasto. Remember, however, that whenever you paint a light tone over a dark one, the undertone will come through in time. Always make important changes in isolated tempera and scrape away the dark paint if possible.

It is very important to work color glazes over these built-up whites to bring them in harmony with the substance of the form. So often they look like plaster highlights. Many of the old pictures look as though there were no color on the form in the light because the restorers have stripped the glazes off the built-up whites.

You may achieve the effect you want with two or three glazes over a positively sculptured underpainting, as El Greco did. You may start with a nebulous underpainting and define the form later with clinching color-textures, as Renoir did. You may start with a colored tone drawing on the white gesso, glaze with an opposing warm or cool color, and then build up the impasto lights. Many of Rubens' sketches were made this way. Sometimes he carried them out to complete paintings. You may combine direct painting with glazing by laying in the drawing shadow-tones in transparent paint and building up the colored lights with impasto.

It is always wise to have some colored whites, semi-neutrals, and hues containing white laid out on the palette. The presence of white in the glaze keeps it from getting glassy. Try not to slip into the habit of glazing with raw colors. Beautiful neutral tones, the optical grays, can be achieved by working semi-neutrals over color glazes and vice versa. Don't neglect to use the semi-neutrals on the cool side of the palette.

When glazing with hues and similar neutral colors, it is almost necessary to have some white in the glaze to bring out the color. It helps to keep the glazes from getting dirty and stringy.

The textural quality of the paint itself must be felt. The contrast of transparent and opaque tones must be worked out to suit the texture. Often it is necessary to work quite opaquely on top of the glazes to clinch the form. Don't get so tied down to a procedure in glazing that you are afraid to throw it overboard. Don't get so flattered by the beauty of rich colors that you hate to dig in for the form. Keep your mind on the problem of making tactile form. Use the color-textures to get realization.

Linework

I have been experimenting with the use of colored lines on top of some of my glazed pictures. Lines are symbols in black and white, and if they are different from the general tone of an area they also have color significance.

I like to use linework to give added significance to the surfaces in the light and to increase the sensation of light and shade. It is possible with sets of lines to force the color power of the painting without cutting down the lightness as much as has to be done if the color changes are all indicated with tones. For instance, neutral red lines can be drawn in the shadow of a green form to say something about the surface and shape of the thing without using a dark solid tone, without losing the green color skin. I can draw on the green form in the light with low yellow linework to say positive things about the direction of textural planes. A glaze of low yellow all over the light will not do the same thing.

PAINTING

Rembrandt's rough underpaintings, in which the graphic brush-work describes the textural existence of the form in the light, serve to make significant texture in a similar way. The glazes caught in the interstices of the paint show up the textural planes.

You don't want too definite glazes to work over when you use colored lines. The paint must be dry so you can wipe off lines that don't work well. The lines may be used to say things about planes and textures, carving statements. Or they may say things about the place, say that one thing lies in back of another, that there is light and shade there. Generally, semi-neutral and neutral lines work more subtly than those of full color.

Sets of lines can say something about the direction and nature of the light. They are used by great fresco painters as a sign for shade. I always think of shade as being full of light. That is why I like to use the word *shade* rather than light and shadow. Shade seems to play over the thing, envelop it, better define it, while shadow seems to fall on the thing and stain the surface with darks.

Strong outlines are usually unnecessary in painting. Drawn lines on the surface give texture and help to create the existence of the solid form. Outlines are a compromise in place of a real consciousness of the form rounding away from the eye to the side that is out of sight.

I do not advocate the use of linework in painting unless the artist feels a need for that kind of realization. If you get strong enough realization without using linework then it becomes super-fluous. The painting will look like a complete aquatint that has been worked over in etched lines. The lines look wiry, stand off the surface. Nevertheless, I do believe that more use could be made of linework. And I firmly believe that the Titian who made great pen drawings could have made marvelous use of line texture on flesh painting. Signorelli laid in his forms with tones and then drew on them with positive linework. His things are certainly among the most powerfully realized paintings in existence.

Some of the paintings I have made with linework do not photograph well. It is very difficult to get the cool underpainting, the tone glazes, and the linework to photograph harmoniously. Many paintings do not photograph well even with the proper color screens, but it doesn't necessarily mean that the work lacks a fine black and white design. A photograph of a painting is a poor thing at best. Surely a painting that could not be photographed would be an exclusive piece of creative art.

Quality of Paint

Whether working in direct paint, or glazing with transparent films over an opaque underpainting, do not forget the qualities of pigments as a means of getting textural realization. Things that are inharmonious technically may do a great deal in a very subtle way to destroy the sense of existence and color relations.

If a painting is all done in translucent colors it is apt to look milky. If all the tones are transparent it will look glassy. If all the tones contain white, as in most direct painting, the work has a tendency to look chalky. It is for this reason that many Cézannes look as though they were made of plaster. One of the greatest difficulties in direct painting is to get the proper changes in the black and white scale working with the color intervals.

When you want to change from one tone to another it is very important to know how much more or less white you need, or if you want to change that factor in the tone at all. It is one of the great stumbling blocks to fine color.

The sense of continuous substance is lost and the quality of light is choked when the painting is not harmonious technically. If one form is painted directly, and another glazed, they will not stay in the same place.

It is wise to have some system in building up a picture. Rubens used to load up the lights impasto, and keep the shadows transparent. I often prefer to glaze the impasto whites with transparent color to get full luminosity, and scumble the shade areas.

It is entirely a matter of relationship whether the tones in a particular canvas work well together. If the shadow side looks dense it may be brought to life by some light opaque marks. Or it may be made to look lighter by some crisp transparent glazes. Perhaps the real trouble is not there but in the light side, which may be too transparent, or too milky, or not sufficiently realized. It may be just a change from transparent to opaque paint that will turn the edge of a contour.

A Holbein or Ruisdael is equally realized everywhere. Rubens made the thing most real at the culminating corner, between the light side and the shadow side. I prefer to emphasize the realization in the light and let the form, the textural detail, relax in the shadow.

In Rembrandt's portrait of a man in a gold helmet the texture of the helmet is most strongly realized in the light, where the hammered metal is built up in the underpainting. The glazes over this are very transparent and full in color. The shadows of the metal are transparent and translucent, to get the quality of the shiny surface. The flesh is glazed underneath with scumbles and top-surfaced with opaque marks and transparent glazes. This contrast in technique brings out the difference in textures and adds to the livingness of the result.

Figure Painting

Almost all flesh is in the yellow-orange scale. If you include Indians and Negroes you can say that any figure lies between red-orange and yellow-orange. The reason for brushing aside realistic human coloring is to say something that isn't tame, more graphic.

You cannot have too much practise in painting the figure just in black and white, or with white, burnt sienna and blue hue. Many studies with palettes limited to the earth colors and blue are invaluable in training the student to draw with paint. You may work directly or underpaint with terre verte and other hues.

The figure is essentially one color. Remember that when you notice a phenomenon, such as the darkness of a man's weather-beaten face above the collar line. Decide on a formula of tone intervals to paint the flesh in each study. Keep the continuity of the complexion, include your exaggerations.

Remember that the arm is the same color on both sides, that both arms are the same color. If you want to make one project more than the other, use color sequence; but do not observe visual perspective in the drawing. For instance, if you have a general flesh color of raw sienna and white, you can modify that color with a little full yellow-orange for the projecting arm, and with ver-million for the receding arm. The general color will look the same. Carry out the change in color in the color intervals; stick to the formula you have decided on for the complexion.

The whites of the eyes are much closer to flesh color than you would suspect. Paint them with the underlying flesh tone. Use different color-textures on the eyeball and the skin to bring out the color contrast.

When the model has been posing for some time the blood runs down to the extremities and gives the flesh a red-purple look. Don't imitate the color. You can observe the change in color quality. It helps to make the figure rise if you consciously paint it more rose at the bottom moving toward yellow in the upper parts. Support this with color sequence in the background.

Don't draw between the fingers and toes with black. Feel those forms as part of the hand or foot. Draw with colors that partake of the color nature of the flesh. A semi-neutral red or orange will define the form without breaking up the plane. Use color se-quences, drawing between the near fingers with more advancing colors.

There is a relative yellow in the flesh, a yellowishness. In a rosy figure it might be painted with a move from light red to a semi-neutral yellow-orange. The greenishness in flesh complexion is really a move toward low yellows. Semi-neutral reds look purple against orange tones. Likewise, the blues of flesh color are neutrals of the orange scales which carry as positive color-changes because of simultaneous contrast.

When you want to get a cool figure you don't have to move to blue. A contrast of alizarine glazes on a terre verte underpainting can look cool.

The figure is influenced immensely by the background. To bring out angles in the figure, put angles in the background. Do the same with curves. In color, use red to bring out rose in the figure, and so forth. But do not neglect the use of contrast.

A piece of drapery is like a necktie, hot stuff to paint, and one of the easiest things for a painter to kid himself into thinking he can do. Don't be fooled by the color. Go after the shape and character. Hew the forms together with colored tones.

Highlight culmination is a poor substitute for plastic performance. Don't hesitate to put a color dark in the light, to bring the form into existence.

The easiest place on the figure to achieve existence is on the knee. The hardest place, the torso. You have to come to grips with the form. It is easy to do it by running to recognizable reds and oranges, but it can be done with other color scales.

I think a photograph of a rugged piece of sculpture is a most edifying thing to a painter interested in realization. Look at an Epstein. It has twice as much modelling as the thing in nature. Notice the amount of dark texture in the light.

CHAPTER VIII

LANDSCAPE AND MURAL

A LANDSCAPE IS THE PORTRAIT OF A PLACE. The face of the earth is an adequate and dignified inspiration for very great works of art. It is not necessary to paint contemporary life, the American Scene, or historical events to produce living contemporary art. Ruisdael, Poussin, Constable, Courbet, Cézanne, and Renoir found nature alive and vital. Of course, you must paint the life around you, paint the things that you know. For one person that may mean the streets of New York, to another it may be a Kansas farm. Social movements may interest some, portraits still others. Chardin found life in china mugs and the fruit on his breakfast table. Yet his compositions are monumental and the realization of his forms intense.

To make a good landscape you must sense and express the scale of things. A few rocks may be as important as a mountain range if you get a fine relationship between the texture of rocks and foliage and surrounding forms. Plastic measures as well as a sensitive selection of things varied in size and shape are vital elements.

Don't walk miles looking for a "subject", somebody else's subject. Look down the road and use your imagination. Get some excitement from the reality in front of you, the geometry of the forms. Get a kick out of the textures of materials. Nature is full of plastic measures, textural measures, color measures: the delicacy of grass tufts, the rough surface of sandy earth, worn round rocks, the bulk of river banks, the character of running water, the quiet passage of mountains against the sky, the fullness of clouds.

Feel the power of nature, the force that threw up mountains

and urges plants to grow. Feel the sunlight and wind. Keep your humanity. Get the nerve of life in your line when you are describing inorganic things.

Get the volume of the hills. Don't just caricaturize the forms. There can be an element of homely humor in a landscape. It is a very subtle thing.

A poetic painting of a fog on a moor is just about the limit in "no-thingness." Poetic in the "ic" sense. Poetic in the sense of Whitman is something else entirely. He was dealing with things, things used as symbols.

In what you now dislike, even hate, lies your advancement to greater understanding. If you get my meaning you will see that I am talking not only about works of art, but things you see in nature. Subjects that don't seem to have meaning for you now may come to interest you if you think about them. Things that seem ugly may come to mean beauty to you.

I like to paint the landscape in the Southwest because of the fine geometrical formations and the handsome color. Study of the desert forms, so severe and clear in that atmosphere, helped me to work out principles of plastic design, the low relief concept. I like the colors out there. The ground is not covered with green mold as it is elsewhere. The piñon trees dot the surface of hills and mesas with exciting textures. When you see a green tree it is like a lettuce against the earth, a precious growing thing. Because the air is so clear you feel the reality of the things in the distance.

A landscape may be conceived very formally, as in a Poussin, or with a more intimate point of view, as in a Renoir. Cézanne was most of all concerned with painting solid forms, the architecture of the place. His pictures often lack texture, some look like colored plaster. Courbet on the other hand, sought to get the difference in quality of rock and earth, foliage and water. He did it with drawing and color and the very texture of the paint.

Ruisdael is perhaps the greatest landscape painter of them all. He carried out a completely realized design, formally composed and yet with a great feeling for the reality of things. You feel the character of individual trees, the textures of bark against grass. His marines are so rich in concept and full of wise observation of the sea; yet simply painted. He knew what happened to waves in a storm and knew how to paint water as a solid form. His skies are real, substantial, yet full of light. It takes great mastery to put over such a fully realized concept of nature without losing the design and mood of a place.

In a Renoir landscape the form is not equally realized everywhere. He says something about the nebula of a group of trees, the feeling of a place bathed in sunlight. Then he gets hold of a corner, comes to grips with the forms, snaps the things into realization. Renoir let the thing relax and then brought it out into culminating points. Some parts of the design were more exciting than others and he wanted to focus on them.

The drawings of Dürer and Breughel are chockfull of knuckly remarks about rocks and trees and clouds. But under all the detail is a large design.

Some Constables are full of textural detail, and in others he condensed the minor forms to emphasize the design. You must find your own way to see nature, whether in detail or in the large design.

Van Gogh saw nature differently. But his work doesn't look the way nature looks. He used what he saw as a point of departure for an exciting design. He drew in color, but his colors are an enlargement of the color relations he saw in nature. His linear technique is used to separate color and shape.

Look at one of Corot's Italian landscapes. It may be a study only fourteen by ten inches in size, but how architectural the composition is. What beauty of scale and fine tonality! The sensitive gradation of tone intervals, his control over them, has something to do with the quality of the light. The color quietly important.

Study the great brush drawings of the Chinese and Japanese. Observe their conventions for perspective, form, texture. When we try to imitate those conventions we lose the content, because those artists were part of an ancient tradition. Our tradition changes rapidly, our schools of thought come to fruition quickly and decay again. We see differently. As Walter Pach has said, "Orientals search for the ideal, occidentals for the particular." Our forms no longer have any philosophical symbolism, and that is a kind of symbolism which when borrowed is an empty thing.

I think it is best to do landscape trom nature at first, to become familiar with the forms. You may make careful studies on the spot and re-do the composition in your studio, but get the sculptural rhythms from nature.

Select the things you like. No great painter ever set out to say that he loved every square inch of the subject he was painting.

The artist looks at a mountain and sees a picture. The cowboy looks down at a canyon and thinks of how many days it would take him to get across it on a pack mule. We need to get more of that concern with distance, as being made of tangible obstacles not vapor, into our work.

You don't need to paint haze and atmosphere to get distance in a landscape. Use the symbols of line, tone, and color. If you want to observe the haze at the horizon, paint the hills as real forms and then paint the haze around them. Or state the forms more delicately than those in the foreground, but no less firmly.

Some perspective is almost always necessary in drawing landscape. But be careful to resist perspective in the foreground. Remember that the closer things are to you the more they are distorted in size. Think of the things in the foreground as being in one plane, those in the middle distance in another plane, and so forth. Use change in scale between the planes as a sign for recession. It is so powerful that you can draw things ten miles away as though they were half an inch back of the forms in the foreground, and the back things will stay back.

Use changes in texture and color to make things project and recede. If you have a bush in the foreground the same size as a hill in the background, make it a positively different material. Let some planes slip off into the shadow, bring others up into the realization of the light.

Get light in the picture by keeping your shadows light. Dense shadows destroy both the form and the sense of light. If a cast shadow doesn't help to define a plane, or function in the design, it has no value except to tell the time of day and the source of light.

Study the way things grow, how they are made. A weed grows like a tree, only in its own character. The principles of growth are the same. Feel the roots in the ground, the rise of the trunk, the radiation of the branches, the weight and delicacy of foliage. Observe the difference between a rigid tree trunk and the giving line of vines and weeds. Study the formal nature of the whole plant and its related parts. Know why an elm tree is different from a pine.

When a great draughtsman like Daumier wanted to draw a tree in an illustration he didn't have to rush out to the country to see nature. His memory was stored with the observations of many trees. He knew how they looked under different conditions, in wind and rain. He knew the character and smell of the forest. And he knew how to represent the kind of tree he wanted in any position or place because he was familiar with the forms.

Go after the character of natural forms, the humble and grand character of nature. Be sensitive to the proportions and changes. Select the fine relations and eliminate the accidental ones. Correct what you see by your mental image of the normal thing.

If you set up new rhythms in place of those in nature, which in some cases is a fine thing, they must be sufficiently distinguished to warrant the license. Sense the dignity of things.

Have a special interest, a positive prejudice about some clump of trees or one particular knoll, an excitement about them that can spread through the whole composition, and so fire the rest of the things that you are only mildly interested in.

Think about a stone wall as you would about a crowd of people. Get the big planes, sides, top and the bottom that rests on the ground. Build it out of the earth, make it a heavy thing. Then pick out the gesture of the wall, describe the rocks that make it. Hew the shapes of those stones, get the sharpness and granular surfaces, get the worn-down, settled-into-place quality.

Don't think of the sea as color. Make it a solid that can support a boat. Think of "wetness" as color-texture.

Study cloud formations. Don't be satisfied with rococo, Spencerian clouds. Observe the flat bottoms of heavy rain clouds, the fine patterns of mackerel skies. Hope to be able to paint clouds in a picture without having them in front of you. Use them to design.

When I used to paint landscapes directly, after selecting the subject I would take half an hour to set my palette. Then I would pick up those set tones and draw with paint. Instead of imitating the colors in nature, I decided on some quality of color that interested me and set a limited palette, with which I could represent relative greens, reds, and other colors. Using such set palettes I could work very quickly, and often made two 26" x 32" canvases a day.

When painting landscape in the mixed technique, it is best to make a small study in direct paint first. It gives you a memorandum of the color composition, with some color relationships inspired by the subject. Sometimes I make a drawing on the spot and work up the underpainting in my studio. I come back to the subject and glaze it from nature. If the underpainting is made out of doors with the idea of glazing in the studio, I make it in semi-neutrals and hues that will remind me of the color when I am away from the subject. I always make written notations of the colors: the fundamental local color tones, the color-textures, and jot down some ideas for the use of color sequences—some prattle about my feeling for the scene.

It is tradition to repeat some foreground color in a blue sky to keep it from falling out of the picture. Some modifications toward green, orange, red, will work subtly to make the sky more palpable. It is better to paint the sky as a solid back drop than an air pocket of blue color. See how Veronese used geometrical rhythms in the sky to complement the design of large figure compositions.

Don't mix pure white in the sky to lighten it. That makes it look opaque. Use white with a little orange or yellow-orange, and so forth. Use whatever color change will help to make the horizon line a place where the form passes back rather than a painted edge.

The bluish purple haze you see in trees is just a neutral green, which seen next to a green that contains more orange or yellow, looks bluish or purplish.

It is a very poor habit to pull all colors back with blue. Bluishness all through the canvas is a sign for atmosphere. The neutrals of any color scale will pull a tone down toward neutrality.

You can use a great range of color sequence to make signs for distance. A green in the foreground can be made to look like yellow-green when placed in the background among cooler and more neutral tones. You can paint a brown field all the way from semi-neutral yellow to semi-neutral red.

Plan the color sequences. If you have a fence in the foreground, fields in the middle distance, mountains and sky in the background, use some arbitrary color changes. Let the fence be in the yellow scale, the fields orange, the mountains with some low red notations, some purples in the sky. The colors do not have to be full intensity to make the sequence work.

It is too easy to get in the habit of letting the distance fade away in pale neutral tones. Remember that you have the whole gamut of the black and white scale to work with as well as the powers of color change. You can put positive colors in the background if you hold them there with more advancing colors and greater realization in the front planes.

Murals

I don't see why any artist who is at all accustomed to graphic expression couldn't draw up some sort of plan for a mural. A feeling for geometrical design, a knowledge of form sufficient to carry things out on a large scale, and technical ability are necessary. A conscious use of foreshortening helps to give plastic realization to a design which must be seen from a considerable distance.

Too many artists are trying to paint their own pictures. There should be more emphasis on the apprentice system practised in the old days. In the average art school a student has no opportunity to study with a master artist who is working out the problems of mural design. Too much theory about the technique of mural painting doesn't get one anywhere. Practise on the wall is what counts.

Under the old atelier system boys were apprenticed in workshops to learn their trade. They were educated not only as craftsmen, but in draughtsmanship, mathematics, architecture, engineering, and many other things. If a boy showed no talent he did the work of preparing panels, grinding colors, tracing working cartoons, and so forth. Those with some ability became assistants, and were allowed to fill in underpaintings from the master's sketches.

Some of the assistants specialized in painting animals, figures, still lifes, or architectural backgrounds. I sometimes say that Rubens must have had an assistant who did nothing but paint fingers and toes. Such details in his work are almost too well done. That remark is an aside, and is in no way meant to belittle Rubens' method of working. I seriously believe that we must have some return to the Renaissance system of education before we will have a healthy tradition of art once again. The artist who wishes to paint small pictures for himself could not get a better fundamental training than by working as an assistant to a master painter. A musician does not attempt to compose sonatas or symphonies until he has had years of training in theory and practise with his instruments.

The government projects have done a great deal to stimulate mural painting in the last few years. Unknown artists have had an opportunity to get experience and do the kind of work that interested them. Small cities and villages have put some kind of art on the walls of their public buildings. It has awakened the public's interest in art, and that is a healthy thing.

Some of the best things have been done by local artists. That is what happened in Italy. Paolo da Francesca was just a native boy painting his home town church in Arezzo.

After all, why be so fearful lest a wall painting be not good. The point is to get the painting on the wall. If fifty artists have a chance at the walls there is a greater probability of getting five great murals than if only five artists are commissioned at high prices. Then let the people decide. Perhaps have the walls repainted every ten years. That is what they did in the old days. Didn't Michelangelo paint his *Last Judgment* on top of a Perugino? Not that we are glad to have lost the Perugino. It just isn't a good idea to think mural painting is sacred because it is big.

The American Indians have a fine sense of geometrical decoration. It would be a grand thing if they could develop a school of mural painting with as little outside criticism as could be. From their first efforts in that direction it is obvious that you have only to give them the wall and they soon learn how to cover it.

Rivera and Orozco assimilated the European tradition and then came back to paint in their native land. It is an amazing thing that they were able to combine their own racial tradition of art with that of the European, and produce great work in such a short space of time. Such an assimilation often takes centuries. I am proud to say that the work of our Indians and the Mexican artists was first shown in the United States by the Society of Independent Artists in 1920 and 1923, respectively.

My own experience in mural painting is very recent. This winter I painted a mural for the Treasury Department for the Bronxville, New York, Post Office. After making a color study to scale, I threw this up on the canvas with a projector. Studies of details such as hands and faces were also thrown up with the projector. Note that I did not put any photograph in the projector but only drawings which were made as mental concepts. In this mural I worked out problems of foreshortening with great care. The railroad train which recedes into the picture is drawn with acute foreshortening. The further you walk from the canvas, the more the cars stretch out in ordinary visual perspective. The horse drawn face-on could not possibly be seen by the eye in that way. One trouble with a great many contemporary artists who are using photographs for documentary detail, is that they are drawing directly from the photograph—repeating all the visual distortions.*

Another criticism I find is that the color in many of our present day wall paintings is meager and timid. This may be the reasonable consequence of a desire to be inoffensive to varied tastes. Another characteristic is a kind of melancholy spirit, maybe this is the real spirit of the time. Still we must be thankful that we have this healthy art infant in the United States and give it room to grow. Above all we must not take away its bottle.

---

*It might be well to remind you that when you look at an average reduced size reproduction or photograph of a painting your eye is seeing it at what would be a considerable distance from the original. Viewing a print six inches wide of an original picture six feet wide from a distance of eighteen inches is the same as looking at the original from a distance of eighteen feet!

CHAPTER IX

MEMORANDA

A Word to the Aesthetic Consumer

I HAVE SAID that the language of art is similar to that of music or literature, the technique of which can be learned. Moreover, I believe that anyone who seeks real enjoyment of art or music must have some knowledge of the language, just as we study grammar in order to learn how to read and write.

The fact that the grammar of art, the use of graphic symbols to make visual images, has been lost to the general public and even the artists during the past hundred years or so, has built up a feeling of mystery around art. The devices of art, the tools of expression, are no more mysterious than are the words of everyday speech. Those few artists who have carried on the tradition of concept-painting, have had to contend with ignorance on the part of public and critics. The making of art has been regarded as an eccentric act, rather than a normal function of primitive and civilized man.

The thoughts and technical means set down in this book represent the experience of one individual, and are therefore not intended to be comprehensive or authoritative. I make little claim to original thought, but rather wish to pass on what I have become conscious of.

It is true both for the consumers of art as well as the producers, that knowledge of the technique must be assimilated before we are free to enter into communication with the author's concept. A knowledge of words increases the enjoyment and understanding of prose or poetry. That one's interpretation will be keener is of little importance; the vital point is that we are enabled to appreciate the meaning because our own grasping of the idea passes through a process similar to that of the creator. Thus, a conscious study of art increases the appreciator's ability to derive spiritual nourishment.

The artist has a creative attitude toward other works of art. His life is enriched by the good things he finds in the world, nature or art. His critical attitude is constructive. He goes through life picking out the worthwhile, using his critical sense to discard the things which are poor and false. This charitable attitude toward the inevitable faults in a living thing permits the artist to enjoy all kinds of work. The minor critic, on the other hand, is so pleased with himself for finding faults that he is unable to appreciate the underlying quality of a work.

Consumers of art make a great mistake in attempting to imitate the "authorities". They are deluded when they think that the evaluation of faults in a work corresponds to appreciating it. I might go so far as to say that the ignorant person who says, "I like that picture,"—even if it is a bad painting—is getting more æsthetic enjoyment out of it than a sophisticated person who is merely looking for the faults. Perfection in a work of art is no criterion of real value because technical perfection is the only standard on which there can be agreement; creative thought, breadth of understanding and its communication to others, is something which cannot be measured.

The integrity of the work is what counts. A brief sketch or a humble study that conveys a sincere thought is more to be admired than a grandiose attempt to imitate a superficially important picture. The artist who knows that he is honestly following his own talent is happy in his work. He feels himself part of the stream of art and is content with his ability, whether he is contributing important original work or only carrying on the tradition.

The consumer and buyer of art would do well to cultivate this frame of mind. With some understanding of the technique and the courage of one's convictions, less importance would be attached to the "success" of the best press-agented names. The true consumer is like the creative artist. He observes, studies, and digests; his perceptions are quickened and his taste is fortified by real knowledge. He is then able to enjoy a work of art for what it is, a document of human, spiritual communication.

I do not recommend that the consumer should study the technique of art all at once, and then feel equipped to understand. He should do as the artist does: seek knowledge when and where he feels the need of it, assimilate it, use it, and then study again.

Sundry Suggestions

(Inspired by twenty-four years of looking at students' pictures)

Go buy yourself a lemon and a plate. You will learn more about painting in five weeks by yourself than in five years in class.

Thomas Eakins used to tell his students to paint an egg, a lump of sugar, and an earthenware plate on a plain linen towel. We need to do more of that kind of studying into the real nature of form and texture, the problems of painting things as we know them.

If you become discouraged, work on another canvas for a while. Don't give up or throw away your failures. Sometimes you can come back to them with a courage you don't have on a canvas that is going well.

Have the courage to begin each day by scraping. If you are glazing, do not hesitate to clean off the color and re-draw the form in tempera.

If you are interested in copying, go to the museum and do it. All the masters learned by copying. I would like to be able to come to class one week, and demonstrate how Rubens painted, Rembrandt the next, and so forth. I should be able to do it.

A sketch should be carefully painted with a great deal of

thought. The color is of least importance and made too much of.

Analyze your motive for painting a study. Studying is thinking, but the adding up of facts is not necessarily thinking. A good study is a search into the nature of the thing and the problem of expressing it in graphic medium.

Don't confuse painting the thing exactly the color you know it is, with painting the thing as it looks.

Before you start to paint come to some conclusions about how you are going to see the color. Have a prejudice about the color. Form a campaign on your palette. Mix up some positive tones and draw with them. Do not be led astray by the casual color-changes you see in nature.

Sculpture the thing with broad tones, tones well separated in interval. Hammer the thing together. The point is to paint firmly. Knit the tones together to make the form and the place it is in. Stroking in shadow-shapes isn't constructive painting. Get the plastic inter-play of tones that will make the dry reality of substance.

I don't know why a square plinth isn't the best thing in the world from which to paint a column.

Find the most realized place in the canvas, and try to realize the rest of it as well. Find the change, the step in interval that will turn the corner, vitalize the form.

Keep up your black and white courage in painting. Interpret the black and white darks of a drawing into colored darks. Have the courage to strike the color notes hard. Think of them as musical octaves—high, low, middle.

Get some bitterness of color-change. Colors don't clash when they can be made to work together on the form. Look out for saccharine colors. Get the textures harsh enough to realize the form.

Bear in mind the color quality you want, and draw into your tones with sequences and changes of value that you have decided on with mental conviction. Organize your thoughts and materials.

If the color is too strongly imposed, not part of the form, it will be more important than the form. Any color will look like a stain when it is out of place. The right color keeps its place on the proper plane.

Look out for crude whites and raw color. They stand out as paint areas. Don't flounder around in color. It is worse than bad language. Use it step by step to build form.

You cannot conquer wrong color with right. It is a matter of good thinking. Think of the neutral colors as carrying the form, the positive colors as color-textures. You lose the significance of the neutrals if you start with positive colors and paint them out.

I am no longer attracted by what the clever brush does. Breadth of thought and not breadth of brushwork is what counts. Broad brushstrokes can record a narrow mind. Crude niggling also may have no breadth of thought.

Avoid graceful wavy brushstrokes. Look out for the one that is too suave in its movement, juicy with paint, like some horrible person in a crowd. The commercial brushstroke.

Keep your mind on the sculptural solidity of the thing, the cubism of the form. A brushstroke describing the shape of the thing, a vital, daring brushstroke is good. But the invention of a brushmark shape isn't invention.

Van Gogh's paint is always drawing. Each mark of the brush is significant. You may think that he tossed his paintings off very casually, but let me assure you that he must have scraped many areas over and over again before getting the drawing to suit himself.

Small brushwork is an endless job if you have no idea what you are after. Men like Chardin or Vermeer may have worked many months on one canvas, weaving tone into tone and building up textures with the utmost care. They never lost sight of the things they were after. A Memling is fresh, though studded with detail.

MEMORANDA

Draw with the brush. Carve the form. Don't be carried away by subtleties of modelling and nice pigmentation at the expense of losing the form.

Every inch of the canvas is important. What you insist on calling a background and think of as a place to get covered with paint —that is a place, a real thing. The surface is no less real than an arm covered with hair and freckles. The background must be a plastic support to the foreground.

Because you see a bland, light-swept area in nature there is no reason for having one on your canvas. There is no change in the solidity of the thing when the light strikes it. The form and color are there.

Some pictures look like brush-developed photographs: clouding of one tone into another; the eye saying "Yes, but"; oiliness; pictures full of gray air, hazes, fogginess, slime; no concern with the dry existence of things, the definition of things. Even water has a definite form and surface. Get the "thereness" of fog or steam. Atmosphere in a painting is nine-tenths fear.

A tone that floats through the canvas like mist over a marsh destroys the dry sculpture of the forms. You may be able to get rid of that pervading smokiness by making one or two positive modifications. The problem is to find out where that tone is cropping out once or twice too often. In a picture which is painted with a close tonality, the modifying color that weaves through the design to hold it together, must be very carefully controlled.

On the other hand, when you are working with positive contrasts of color, the color harmony may be thrown out of key by mis-related values in the black and white scale. It is always wise to keep tones set on the palette which have been arranged in intervals that will function properly on the canvas.

Little highlights sprinkled onto the canvas cheapen the concept. One or two well selected textural accents will bring life to the whole composition.

Some paintings have no color, no sense of the twelve colors. A fine painting always gives one the feeling of color powers in reserve, even if it is painted with only vermillion and blue. A painting without color quality would make one feel that vermillion and blue were the only colors in the world; one wouldn't feel that there were also yellow and green and purple on the palette which the artist had not chosen to use in the particular canvas.

While I am not at all interested in color for itself, I am a little tired of these half-dead color schemes constantly repeated by so many contemporary painters. One feels that all the colors are pulled down by black. I call them chain-gang pictures. "Give us light red, Indian red, and black," they say. "Give us the ball and chain." I like to see my students practise with the palette of hues and then open it up, use the force colors. You can't get powerful color-plastic realization without using the whole gamut of the palette.

There are students who, when painting heads, come to the cheek with a loud whoop and plant a rose there. "I know what color this is going to be! This is a red cheek and that is yellow hair!" Be sure of the colors that are less obvious. I would be perfectly willing to make a study in neutrals and let someone else paint in the blues and reds.

There are others who find oil paint romantic. Their palettes looks that way. By a romantic palette, I mean they have no control over it. Well, Delacroix was what they called a Romantic, and he had absolute control over his palette. He had an orderly palette, set, tuned for work. In fact, it was the job of one of his assistants to set the palette every morning. Could one imagine a musician tuning the piano every time he was going to play? To play your colors by eye is worse than playing the piano by ear.

Some canvases are immersed in color. They exist as spots of color and not as forms. Stuttering color vibrations do not contribute to the realization of the thing, because they are not put in purposefully. In the work of Seurat, you can see the dots of neutral colors carrying the form and then the dots of more intense color that make the color-texture. It is a totally different principle than that of the Impressionists who used broken color to imitate visual effects.

Don't imitate the color in nature. Of what use is it to get the colors that a perfected camera could record more accurately than the human eye?

When you find that your work is losing clarity of structure and sensitivity, some study of fine architecture may help to discipline your thought. If you feel that your pictures are suffering from over-stylization, artificial simplicity, observe things in nature with great care. Forget that you are looking for picture material. Perhaps describe the forms to yourself as though planning to write. Refresh your concepts of things, your archetypes, by looking at nature not as something to be analyzed into geometrical shapes but as a world of interesting things. Observe the texture and character of places and people as any human being would, without thinking of how you would transcribe your thoughts into paint. All vital work springs from a background of human observation.

There is no ideal balance which the artist should cultivate between his interest in art and nature. The creative process is an organic thing which cannot be dissected. An artist's way of working is regulated by his individual personality. The problem of expressing what his mind and heart see in nature must be knit with the problem of formal expression, while he is working. At other times he may be more aware of nature than the means and end, and vice versa. When there is lack of coördination between the object, the mind, and the hand, there is no concept and no art results. The work will only be scientific or emotional observation, or abstract formula.

The artist has many problems to solve in his life. He must grapple with economic difficulties as well as human and artistic ones. It is indisputable that modern life offers little encouragement to the fine artist. On the other hand, obstacles of some sort seem to be a necessary incentive to creative work. If the artist is free to work all the time, the work is apt to go up a tree. Only a strong personality seems able to survive the privilege of having unlimited leisure.

When you are too satisfied with your own opinions, when you find your work growing stagnant, arouse your interest by looking in new directions. Change your medium, look for new subject matter, or go to the museum.

Sometimes we come to a fresh appreciation of the great masters through a sympathy for the work of lesser ones. If we are sensitive to the real principles of art, we get a kick out of finding them in work that previously has passed our notice. This ability to grow within ourselves is a vital quality. Without it there is no chance of maturing. Question your own judgments, which include those you have accepted from others.

We are so apt to form generalizations which prevent us from finding new sources of information and inspiration. For instance, there is the idea that the Germans' creative talent is psychologically limited to music and literature. We recognize a few graphic artists like Dürer, Bosch, and Cranach. Why forget that great painter, Grünewald? His work goes far beyond cruelty or sentimentality in its tremendous realization.

Giovanni Bellini is a fine artist whose work is often overlooked because Giorgione and Titian came after him. Carpaccio is another whose contribution has been eclipsed by the importance of his near contemporaries. We too often think of the Van Eyck brothers as inventors of oil painting, rather than artists. The trouble with studying the history of art is that we put tags on an artist's work and forget to renew our acquaintance with it.

It is a deep secret, but Millet really is good. He has been a bad influence because his work was popularized for its pictorial "charm". Underneath the obvious subject matter is grand plastic design and profound feeling for character. Théodore Chassériau is important in his relation to Ingres and Delacroix.

I mention these examples to point out a matter of principle. You can often find your own direction and means through the work of lesser, but no less genuine, masters. Botticelli, Watteau, the Le Nain brothers and the like may help you more than Michelangelo and Leonardo. Find your own direction and follow it through.

There is a real necessity for work done today to convey the artist's spiritual and material contact with this time. What importance can your work have if you take a point of view and technical method which if you should succeed in doing ten times better than you could hope to do, would then be one tenth as well done as it was done four hundred years ago?

CHAPTER X

NOTES ON PAINTING TECHNIQUE

ANYTHING YOU PAINT underneath another tone is bound in time to come through to some extent. The most opaque pigments are really translucent and become more so as the binder changes with age.

Since the oil binder of pigments darkens with time, you should paint on a white ground which can reflect light through the layers of oil paint and counteract their darkening as the paint grows more transparent.

A white gesso ground made of glue and whiting retains its brilliance longer than an oil ground. Pictures painted on panels stay more brilliant than those on canvas because the gesso is thicker.

All paint films contract when they dry. A picture should be painted "fat over lean": the paint that dries fastest and hardest on the bottom, working up to paint that dries slowly in the upper layers.

A layer of oil paint dries with a skin on the top which prevents the paint underneath from drying. Paint dries by oxidation and this skin prevents the underneath paint from breathing.

Varnish dries evenly through the paint film. If there is too much varnish in the paint it may crack and be difficult to paint with, but some varnish should be used in all oil painting so the paint films will dry evenly.

A *good medium for direct painting is*: one part *oil*, one part *varnish*, and one part *turpentine*. Stand oil is better than cold pressed linseed oil. Do not use poppy oil. It may look lighter than linseed oil but it dries very slowly and darkens more than linseed. The addition of a little venice turpentine makes the medium more crisp to work with.

When working directly you should either paint all at one time or build up the paint films very carefully, letting the picture dry between each sitting. Always mix the medium with the tones on the palette, to get even distribution of oil and varnish through the paint films. Add a little more oil to the medium in each successive layer of paint. You have only to look at the direct paintings made in the last sixty years to see how much damage has been done already by the sloppy use of medium. The paint is stained as though with tobacco juice and the paint films are cracking all over.

Get the habit of keeping your palette and brushes clean. Wash brushes every day with a mild soap and dry thoroughly. While working, clean the brush with turpentine and wipe with a rag before making each positive color change. It is a bad habit to get texture by the mere accidental use of a brush full of dirty oil paint. Keep the cup of medium clean. Do not use medium which has been standing open to the air a long time.

When an area starts to "sink" give it a coat of good retouching varnish. Cheap retouching varnish forms a hard film over the paint layer which prevents it from drying.

You should wait at least one year and preferably two before varnishing an impasto oil painting.

There is no really satisfactory varnish. Damar darkens least but it is soft and sometimes becomes sticky in damp weather. Mastic is harder but darkens some and also has a tendency to bloom. Copal dries very hard and becomes insoluble, but darkens a good deal. Because of its insolubility I have often thought of putting a thin coat of it over each of my glazed pictures so restorers would have trouble removing the color as they have done to so many old paintings. A final varnish of damar could be removed easily and renewed without disturbing the protective film of copal.

If a picture has been permanently varnished and you want to do more work on it, you should remove the varnish from the areas you are going to re-paint. If it was done in oil, you can never be sure that the re-painted area will stay in tone with the rest.

Never rub oil over a painting to bring out the color. It leaves a greasy film that will darken. The final varnish brings out the colors, but its real purpose is to protect the oil paint from absorbing moisture from the air. A wax varnish dries mat.

Canvas must be sized with glue to prevent the oil from burning up the fibres. Some chemists say that the canvas should be sized with a hot glue that can penetrate through from front to back. Then it is important to put a coat of varnish or shellac on the back to prevent the glue from absorbing moisture from the air. Moisture is bad for paint films and makes them swell and contract, causing cracking.

Commercial canvas is primed with an oil ground. If you prime your own, use a half-oil ground which will stay whiter.

Gesso grounds for oil painting must be sized to prevent the oil from sinking into the ground, staining it and making putty.

Sketches may be made on paper or cardboard sized with glue or shellac.

Do not use zinc white in oil painting or for tempera. It is very chalky, apt to crack, and requires more oil binder than lead white does. Consequently, it will darken more. Lead white is the most reliable. When ground with oil it becomes like horn after the paint is dry. Titanium white is chemically inert and a very intense white. Sometimes it chalks a little but it is otherwise reliable.

Most oil paints are ground too fine, which reduces the color power and makes the pigment take up more oil. Some pigments are heavier than others and require some filler to keep them suspended in the oil. Too much filler makes the pigment like butter and increases the oil content. (If you have the time and interest, grind your own pigments. Use oil and some varnish.) Always use the materials of a reputable firm. Cheap colors are full of extenders, poor in color power, and will not stay permanent.

Generally speaking, the transparent pigments are ground very fine and take up a lot of oil. The opaque pigments require less oil for easy handling and dry faster. Remember this, and do not put a thick layer of white lead or Indian red over a layer of alizarine, ultramarine, viridian, and other slow drying pigments.

Most of the permanent colors may be mixed together. But alizarine should never be mixed with the earth colors, raw sienna and raw umber. It is considered safe in mixture with burnt sienna and burnt umber, but it is wisest not to mix it with any colors at all. Since it is a very useful glazing color this is important to remember. Doerner says that it may be mixed with cremnitz white, but other authorities disagree with him.

When tube paints contain an excess of oil, this can be removed by squeezing the pigment on a blotter. In about half an hour the superfluous oil will be absorbed.

Gesso Grounds

The old masters generally worked on wood panels which had been well seasoned. These are expensive and hard to obtain so the modern artist uses a wood plyboard or panel of compressed wood fibre. I have used Masonite Prestwood for the past ten years and prefer it to plywood, which has a tendency to crack and warp.

If you use Prestwood, both sides should be roughened with coarse sandpaper. Gesso will chip off a smooth or non-absorbent surface. Both sides of the panel should be sized, and care taken to work plenty of glue into the edges and corners.

Glue has a strong "pull", so there must be an even number of size and gesso coats on both sides of the panel or it will warp. I generally glue theatrical gauze to the back with a strong casein glue, which counteracts the warping as effectively as several coats of gesso. The back may then be coated with shellac or wax.

Because glue paints contract so much, it is important to remember never to put a stronger coat over a weaker one. If you do, the top coat will tear off the underlayers, cracking or peeling like old wall paper.

General proportions for making size: One ounce of rabbit skin glue to eleven ounces of water. (For sizing canvas, one to fourteen.) Good quality white flake glue may be used.

Soak the glue in water overnight and heat in a double boiler. Never let glue boil, as it loses its strength.

Glue is stronger in cold weather than in hot.

A good glue should set to a jelly of stiff consistency. If it separates it has become rancid and is no good. When it is the right strength for size it is tacky when rubbed between the fingers.

If you add a few teaspoons of whiting to a quart of glue it will keep for a long time in a covered container. The whiting keeps the glue from souring.

To make gesso: Add about eighteen ounces of bolted whiting to a quart of warm, liquid size. Whiting makes a tougher gesso than precipitated chalk. A little titanium white may be added to the whiting if you want a very white surface. The amount of whiting may be varied. Stir it into the glue until the liquid looks like heavy cream.

Size the panels on both sides with warm size. Be sure that the size gets into all the pores of the surface. Let the panels dry overnight.

The first coat of gesso should be applied quite warm. If it is rubbed in with a piece of hard turkish towel you will have less trouble with air bubbles. All the air bubbles must be rubbed out, as they form pock holes in the gesso.

The next coat should be put on as soon as the first one starts to dry white. Be sure to add two or three teaspoons of water to each quart of gesso before starting the next coat. This counteracts the loss of moisture caused by evaporation. It is also necessary in order that each successive coat should be slightly weaker than the one underneath.

The first two coats may be put on with criss-crossing brush-strokes. After that, if you are covering a large panel, paint the surface in squares as large as one brush-load of paint will cover easily. Work one coat in one direction, and the next coat at right angles to it.

After the first three or four coats use a medium fine piece of sandpaper to get rid of specks of dirt and other foreign substances. Add two or more coats and let the gesso set. When the surface is dry to touch, go over it with a fine sandpaper to get rid of irregularities. If you like a rough surface, you can put on the last coat or two with a cold gesso. The brushmarks will stand up. Rubens often worked on a gesso with sweeping brushmarks criss-crossed on the surface. Its texture shows through the glazes.

Do not gesso in a cold room. Many air bubbles will arise when the hot gesso comes in contact with the cold surface of the panel. If you dry the panel with too much heat the gesso will crack. The outside surface contracts faster than the layers underneath.

If you have some old gesso saved in a pot and want to know how strong it is, warm it up and paint out two or three coats on a piece of sized wood. Let the sample dry and sandpaper it with OO paper. If the surface becomes very shiny there is too much glue. If it powders very easily there is too little.

Gesso for frames, wooden boxes, and other things which must stand up under hard usage, should be made with a strong size. You can use proportions of one part glue to six parts water. Size the wood well on all sides and let it dry overnight. Add as much whiting to the glue as it will take and apply the gesso hot. Let the first coat dry overnight and then sandpaper. Add a little water to the gesso and put on a second coat. This dries very fast. The surface can be roughened by scratching.

Gesso for canvas must contain some oil (or other plasticizer) to keep it from cracking. Add boiled oil drop by drop to a heavy, cool gesso and beat well until the oil is absorbed. From a quarter to a third oil by volume will make a good half-oil ground. I have sometimes added white lead, stiffly ground in oil and diluted with turpentine, to the regular gesso to make a half-oil ground. Use about four parts gesso to one part oil pigment of equal consistency. Pour the oil paint into the gesso very slowly, and stir well. A half-oil ground should dry several weeks before being used. You can add more oil to the gesso, but why do so as the oil will only make the ground darken like regular oil paint.

Tempera

Water-soluble binders like glue and gum arabic are called distempers. Tempera is an emulsion made of a water-soluble binder and an oily binder. Egg yolk is a natural emulsion and is often used as the base for an emulsion containing oil or varnish. Pure egg tempera is very delicate and difficult to handle. It cannot be used for impasto work.

Casein is another natural emulsion, which has very strong binding power. When used alone as a binder the pigment dries very mat, and becomes waterproof.* It dries so fast that it is easier to handle and more suitable for impasto work if some varnish and oil are added. If too much oil is mixed with casein the paint will yellow.

The advantage of using an emulsion for grinding pigments is that you have the strong binding power of the water-soluble glue (which dries fast and does not darken the way oil does) plasticized by an oil, varnish or balsam. The plasticizer makes the paint less brittle and easier to handle, because it does not dry so fast as distemper.

The beauty of the tempera medium is in its fine dry pastel tones and brilliant colors. It may be applied in delicate washes,

*If you want to make gesso or glue tempera waterproof, give it a coat of formalin (4 per cent formaldehyde).

or built up impasto. The tones can be worked together in subtle gradations, or applied crisply in the finest of detail. It can be used to paint pictures very complete in sculptural detail, as by Mantegna and Signorelli. But if you wish to get great luminosity of color and strong color-textures, it is necessary to glaze over the tempera with transparent oil colors.

The medium has none of the greasy qualities of oil paint. The surface dries quickly, so you cannot push the paint around. At first this seems a disadvantage but it really helps to keep the drawing clear-cut. The tones dry slightly lighter than when the paint is wet. Sets of graduated tones have to be kept on the palette so one can be sure of getting the right tone in the right place on the canvas. Because the binder has a lower refractive index than oil, the pigment layers are more opaque than oil paint of the same thickness. While you are working out the drawing of the form a very thin wash of tempera will cover up tones that are to be changed. If the paint gets loaded up from much re-drawing, it can be scraped off with the palette knife.

An emulsion that contains more than half water-soluble binder may be diluted with water. This is preferable for underpainting. If you want to build up with tempera on top of oil glazes, it is wise to use an emulsion that is soluble in turpentine. In this case, the emulsion is made by adding a small quantity of casein, or other water-soluble binder to the varnish and oil.

One may also make a "mixed white" for underpainting or building up. To do this you grind a batch of white pigment with casein and another with oil. If you want to thin with water, use two parts casein-ground pigment to one part oil-ground pigment, by bulk. Grind them together well with the palette knife or muller. If you want to dilute with turpentine or thin glazing medium, use two parts oil pigment to one part casein pigment. These proportions may be varied slightly. If you mix equal parts the paint is hard to thin and has a tendency to cheese.

It is best to use mixed white for painting on canvas as it has more give than plain tempera. It stays wet a little longer than tempera and permits freer brushwork. Titian and Veronese probably used this medium, perhaps Rembrandt.

A very oily tempera will not stick well on the gesso surface. As the paint tends to crawl, the brush will sometimes pick up the paint underneath. Too much oil in the emulsion will make the paint darken as in regular oil paint.

If you are making an oil-in-water emulsion, add the oil part to the water part. Shake well in a bottle or beat with an egg beater until the mixture looks like mayonnaise. A good emulsion can be diluted with water easily. If the emulsion is to be a water-in-oil combination, put the oil and varnish in the bottle first, and add the glue or egg second.

Casein solution can be made with powdered casein or cottage cheese. It is very important that the casein should be fresh as it loses its strength. It smells sweet when fresh. Take six level teaspoons of powdered casein and stir in two ounces of cold water. Then add four ounces of hot water and one teaspoon of strong ammonia water. (Do not use household ammonia as this often contains other chemicals). Stir the mixture while it effervesces, and let it stand twenty minutes. It should then be translucent and feel tacky like glue when rubbed between the fingers. It should be about the consistency of thin honey. If it feels granular it is no good.

To make a casein emulsion: To two parts casein solution, add one part medium consistency varnish and one-quarter part stand oil. A few drops of venice turpentine will help the emulsion to form quickly. Shake well. This emulsion is quite strong and may be diluted with water for grinding pigments. Always grind a little pigment with a new emulsion and let the sample dry to see if the emulsion has the right binding power. It should not crack when built up in a quarter inch impasto.

The proportions of varnish and oil may be changed, provided you bear in mind that the casein part must be more than the oil part or it will not stay emulsified. If the casein is too watery, it will not accept the oily constituents easily. When the pigment is ground in a good stable emulsion, it stands up like oil paint. There is something the matter with the emulsion if the paint separates into water and pigment, or if the paint curdles.

If you grind the pigments in water first, use a strong emulsion. Otherwise, add a little water to it. When grinding large quantities use a muller and ground glass. Smaller amounts may be ground with the palette knife. Be sure to get the pigment evenly ground.

As tempera dries fast on the palette, large quantities should be kept in covered jars, or muffin tins covered with wet blotters. You can keep the paint on the palette moist by spraying with water every half hour. Do not try to re-grind paint that has dried.

Some pigments require more binder than others, which you can tell from the feeling in grinding. Terre verte is one of these. I prefer to use oxide of chromium with a little raw umber. This has more color power and is less transparent than terre verte.

Pigment can be kept ground in emulsion for some time before it becomes moldy. If a little oil of cloves is added to the emulsion, it will stay sweet longer. Do not keep it in a hot place.

A very simple and practical use of tempera is to mix a jar full of Titanic white* with emulsion, and use all other colors in dry form, in small jars on or near your palette. They can then be quickly brush-mixed with emulsion or white or both.

In using tempera I recommend that the student work first with black and white, or raw umber and white, to get the feel of the medium. A set of tones should be mixed on the palette, say five in number, ranging from white to medium dark. Many studies of the simple solids should be made with this limited means. Then paint with the hues, and work up to the use of the full palette.

*Prepared by Lewensohn Co., N. Y. C.

Lay in the first drawing very thin, and then build up tone on tone until you get the sculptural form as desired. Use sable or bristle brushes, and dilute the paint with water. Learn how to mix from one tone interval to another to make a graduated tone. You have to work quickly and surely, keeping the edge of the tone wet to work the next brushstroke in. You can also modulate tones by hatching. When you are skilful you can match dry tones.

After you have worked out the drawing of the form, keeping the paint very thin, you can start to load up the lights. This gives textural support to the glazes.

If you want to make complete pictures in tempera, you can use the full gamut of the palette, and carry out the drawing in great detail. It is a waste of time to put too much detail in the underpainting, as it is obliterated by the glazes. Details should be added later with a mixed white.

Use your studies for experiments in glazing. Make them in different colors, different tonalities.

When the underpainting is completed, let it dry over night. It must then be "isolated" to prevent the oil varnish glazes from sinking into its semi-absorbent surface. This may be done with gelatin* (one teaspoon of cooking gelatin to six ounces of water). Spray the gelatin on with an atomizer or use a soft brush. You have to work very deftly or the water may dissolve the tempera. Some artists prefer to isolate with a thin damar varnish or diluted shellac. Let the painting dry thoroughly before glazing. Moisture left on the surface may cause blooming.

Glazing

General formula for glazing medium: one part stand oil, two parts heavy varnish, and two to three parts turpentine. This may be adjusted to suit. If there is too much oil the glazes will slide. If there is too much varnish the surface gets too sticky. Too much

*A little grain alcohol added to the gelatin solution will preserve it for future use.

turpentine in the medium will dissolve the under glazes. A few drops of venice turpentine in the medium makes it more precise in handling. The medium should stand several hours after being made up, so the turpentine will be absorbed by the oil and varnish.

Even when glazing you should observe the principle of "fat over lean." If you are putting many glazes on top of one another, add a few drops of oil to the medium now and then.

In glazing, work with as little medium as possible. The blackened blues and madders in the old pictures are caused by an excess of medium. If you are covering a large surface, the glazes should be mixed in jars so an even amount of medium is carried through the paint layers.

If some part of the glazed painting sinks after the second glaze, give it a light coat of retouching varnish or thin damar. When the glazes get too glassy, let the painting dry and rub them down with pumice.

If you build up in white with an oil-in-water tempera on top of the glazes, you must isolate the new areas with gelatin or varnish. It is better to use a water-in-oil tempera or mixed white. They are sufficiently non-absorbent not to need isolation.

You can build up impasto with either white or color. The tempera will work well on wet or dry glazes. A half dry glaze that contains a little venetian turpentine is fine to work into. You can use broad strokes of tempera or the finest hair-lines.

You can also paint thin veils of tempera over whole areas that have gone dead, and then re-draw with solid white. Sometimes I work a little tempera white or dry pigment into a wet glaze to make a scumble. It makes a useful textural contrast to scumbles made of glazes containing white oil paint.

CHAPTER XI

ETCHING, AND DIVERS MEDIUMS

ETCHING IS A WAY OF DRAWING—purely a drawing technique. The line is a symbol which expresses without equivocation the thought of the artist. The beauty of an etched print is in its significant linework used to define and describe things.

A quality of etching, which gives it a special character shared with line engraving, lies in the fact that the ink lines are raised in relief when the bitten plate is run through the press and printed. The raised surface of those lines gives them more textural significance in a very subtle way.

Popular etching in the last century degenerated into the parlor-print type of thing. In Whistler's Venice vignettes we see precious lines surrounded by an expanse of tone, reaching the boutonniere stage, a butterfly in the corner of a plate. I agree with Whistler, however, that it is bad taste to make an etching over ten by fourteen inches in size. As for Zorn's eminent men in line-storms, that use of linework is an imitation of paint marks copying light and shadow shapes.

The classical linework of the masters was used to make things and texture and light and shade. An etching without drawing and composition is nothing, just a technical *tour de force*. Look at the etchings of Rembrandt and the line drawings in *Punch* by John Leech. Any kind of linework you don't find in their work is hardly worth having.

The classical line technique used by engravers before etching was popular is important, but need not be imitated. See how they used sets of parallel lines to define the planes, the direction of the forms. They had formulas for making flat surfaces and curved surfaces. Linework moving in one direction describes one movement of the form, a counter-direction further defines. Wide lines and thin lines, parallel and hatched, textures and dots—all used to sculpture form.

In etching, the line is more sensitive and richer in character than in engraving. In the fine Rembrandt plates there is a great range of texture, from fine drypoint to the clean engraved line; the rich etched line to the velvety line of drypoint with the burr. He used those contrasts significantly, letting the shadow side of the form slip away into fine cross-hatching and bringing out the texture in the light. He used contrast of texture to bring out color, to emphasize the design.

Well-done cross-hatching is made with clean parallel lines so that the interstices are even. The contrast of strongly bitten lines lying over finer ones, positive textures lying over under-textures, gives brilliance to the hatching.

The difference between an etched line and an engraved line is that the etched line is made wider and deeper by acid biting, while in engraving the metal is lifted out of the line by the tool itself. The sides of an engraved line are smooth, those of an etched line are rough, so the latter prints warmer. Different acids bite cleaner lines than others. Dutch mordant makes a straight-sided groove, nitric acid a more horseshoe-shaped and ragged groove. Rétroussage brings the ink over the surface of the line and gives a richer print. When overdone, the line is blurry. Leaving some slight tone on the plate when wiping, enrichens the print. When overdone, the result is melodramatic technique.

You can learn the technique of etching without any great difficulty if you have some feeling for craftsmanship. *The Art of Etching* by E. S. Lumsden is a good book on technique. But there is no end to the problem of drawing with the needle. One needs to make many drawings with pencil and pen. Study the master line draughtsmen: Dürer, Rembrandt, John Leech, Ingres, et al.

It is not a good idea to make an etching from too perfect a drawing. Often a wash or crayon study is more inspiring than one worked out in lines. You have to invent ways to translate the wash textures into line.

I generally make drawings for an etching on transparent paper so I can alter and improve them by tracing. I make the drawing the size of the plate. When I get what I want I transfer the main outlines to the smoked ground. (Vermillion powder rubbed on the back of the drawing makes a nice tracing). I don't like a tracing on the plate that is too full of detail, because I find myself trying to copy the traced lines rather than inventing a concentrated living line to define the things.

Always keep your etching needle properly sharpened to a rounded point that will not tear the surface. Draw with even pressure, bearing down just hard enough to remove the wax ground and to expose the metal beneath. When you draw with uneven pressure some lines will bite faster than others.

After drawing the most important contours and the positive linework that is to sculpture the forms, bite the whole plate in a half water, half nitric acid bath. Most etchers control the strength of the bath with great care and time the biting. I work almost entirely by instinct and judge the depth and character of the biting from experience. Be careful to keep removing the bubbles from the lines which are formed by the action of the acid. Use a feather or brush. Look out for places where the ground may break down, especially where there is a lot of cross-hatching. Where there are the most lines the acid will bite fastest, because heat is generated as the acid attacks the metal, and the acid bites faster when hot. Keep stirring the acid around in the bath. Take the plate out now and then, wash it with water and dry it. Hold it up to the light to see how deeply the lines are being bitten. Also feel the depth of the line with your needle. Only experience in printing can teach you to judge the biting.

When the more delicate lines have been bitten sufficiently, stop them out and bite the rest of the plate a little longer in the bath. Before doing this more lines may be added. After this biting, stop out some more, and fill in further new linework. After some experience with the bath tray biting, try "spit-biting." Apply saliva with a brush to all or such parts of the plate as you wish to bite. The acid is applied with a bulb-topped syringe and poured off after biting. A plate may be finished entirely in this way, in fact most of my etchings were so made. Depending on the difficulties I may run into, I work on the first state a long time, or pull a proof right away. Etching is one long fight to keep the plate under control, and having the courage to scrape out an area if it fails.

Before laying a second ground, be sure that the plate is completely free of grease. Use benzol, followed by the finest bolted whiting and clean water, to clean the plate. Cheap whiting is full of impurities that will scratch the surface.

When you take out an area with scraper, scotch stone, burnisher, and French charcoal, be sure that you get the surface smooth with a good polish. If the hole is quite deep, tap it up from the back, finding the place with calipers.

I generally use a rolled ground, but sometimes prefer a liquid ground in the later states. When you want to remove the ground in one area you can lay the new ground with liquid ground, and do not need to clean off the whole plate. You can make your own liquid ground by dissolving shaved-up ball ground in ether or chloroform. A liquid ground has to be poured very skilfully or it will be thicker on one part of the plate than another.

When a plate is underbitten all over, I sometimes succeed in laying a very thin ground for rebiting all over the surface, something very difficult to do without filling in the lines. Roll out the ground on another steadily heated plate and then deftly pass the roller across the surface of the very slightly warmed etched plate two or three times. You have to examine the plate with a magnifying glass to clean out any lines which may contain ground. Sometimes it is possible to re-ground an underbitten plate if you first fill in the lines with whiting paste. The ground does not stick on top of the lines full of whiting, and the whiting can be washed out with water.

I have always been quite patient about making corrections, like scraping out a line or pushing together the sides of a line that I don't want to hold too much ink. You may sometimes grind down a whole area of linework so it will print more gray than black. It is just a trick if done stupidly, but it can be used to say a lot about light and texture.

Lately, I have been using the graver occasionally. It is a tool that takes a lot of practise to control. To make long, sweeping curved lines that lie parallel requires patience and skill. I like the fine clean line, it has a steely quality.

Making over two hundred plates in the last thirty-five years has not made me an expert technician in etching—perhaps I do not wish to be one.

If you are doing a great deal of etching it is wise to use a small electric fan to blow aside the acid fumes. They are bad for the membranes of the throat and nose, and hurt the eyes.

Printing an etching is almost an art in itself. I do not consider myself a proficient workman in that art. It is a matter of regret that very few young men are practising plate printing for artists. Peters Brothers are gone, Peter Platt also. Charles S. White is one of the old craftsmen still available. The young etcher should have his own press if possible, and from Lumsden's book he should be able to train himself to print quite well.

When you go through a lot of proofs, find the places that are apt to print badly and look for those in each proof. Sometimes the lines don't fill up because the inking-up is not done carefully;

sometimes the ink is pulled out from too much rétroussaging.

John Taylor Arms, that master technician, has most of his plates printed in England, where they have a real tradition of craftsmanship.

As soon as the first print is made an etching begins to wear down, but with modern steel-facing it is possible to preserve the plate through thousands of printings.

Every print is a handmade thing, the personal work of the artist, yet it may be put out in great quantity as a means of reproducing the artist's concept. Such prints might be sold at fifty cents or a dollar. I don't like high prices for prints, and limited editions. They delude the public, who think, the higher the price is, the better the work must be. It keeps people from having the courage to buy the work of unknown artists. But it is hard to convince the dealer that quality in quantity might be a financial success. He demands limited editions, and perhaps he is right. Today there is so much cheap printing of pictures by other means that it may be wise to keep the artist's etching a rarer item.

Aquatints

The English artists are remarkable craftsmen. There is astounding technique in their prints, especially in the aquatints and mezzotints.

I don't much care for an aquatint that is without at least a few etched lines. Without some linework, the print often looks like a poster or an imitation of a painting. There are a few fine Goyas with no etched lines, and then there is Delacroix's magnificent plate of the *Man at the Anvil*. Most of my aquatints started out as etchings. Working on a zinc plate, and not liking the coarse bite of the line, I would decide to continue the work in aquatint. There are but few in my product and, like my etching, they have no technical excellence.

The trouble with aquatint is that, if you mar some area or want to make a change in it, it is so very difficult to patch with a tone anywhere near the particular grain you had before. And each time you remove the surface it takes a good deal of the copper off so you get a deep hollow in the plate which becomes hard to print evenly.

The beauty of an aquatint is in the contrast of textural tones. A tone that just looks like an acid tint isn't anything much worth having. You can do all kinds of things with an aquatint plate besides laying fine and coarse grained tones. You can scrape down a tone to lighten it, as one would with a mezzotint. You can work line textures against tone textures. You can melt the edge of a tone into the plain surface of the plate or you can have sharp contrast of gray and white.

To lay a fine aquatint ground, you should use the box method. Put rosin dust in a closed cardboard box and shake it up thoroughly. If you put the plate in the bottom of the box through a slot in the side as soon as you have finished shaking it, the ground will be coarse, as the large particles settle to the bottom first. If you want a fine ground, let the rosin settle to the bottom for quite a time before putting the plate in the box.

If you are not very fussy about getting an even tone, you can put the rosin in a fine muslin bag. Hold the bag well above the plate and tap on it with a pencil until the rosin sifts down to the plate. If you want a very fine ground, hold the bag high and to one side of the plate, and only the finest particles will drift onto the plate itself.

Handle the plate with a great deal of care so the powdered rosin does not move around on the surface. To make the particles stick on the surface, the plate is heated slightly until the powder becomes shiny and gives off a sweet smell. If you want a coarse ground, heat the plate longer until the specks of rosin spread out to form globules.

When the plate is put in the acid bath, the acid attacks the metal exposed between the grains of rosin. The larger the grains, the larger will be the white specks between the black of the etched parts, in the print. The deeper you bite the plate, the darker will be the tone, because the grooves hold more ink. Naturally, a fine ground looks blacker than a coarse ground, because almost all the surface of the plate is taking ink. If you bite too much, the acid eats under the particles of rosin and the tone will look moth-eaten.

After the ground has been laid on the plate, use stopping-out varnish or liquid ground to block out the areas that are not to be etched. Varnish out, then etch. Repeat this three or four times until the darkest tones are finished. Remove the ground and rosin. A new rosin ground must be laid for each tone that is to be texturally different. When you are very skilful you can lay a ground that graduates from fine particles to coarse particles. This is done partly in the floating of the rosin onto the plate and partly by careful heating.

My own way has been to put in etched lines for the general design before the aquatint tones. More lines may be put in later. It is difficult to draw a clean straight line over a rough aquatint surface, even through the wax ground.

Goya was the great master of aquatint. He designed his plates with broad textural patterns. See how he played finely grained tones against coarsely grained ones; dark tones against lighter ones; even tones against graduated ones. Notice how skilful his edges are, particularly where the aquatint tone is next to the bare plate. See how the light of the bare plate moves into the tone. Sometimes the edges are precise, elsewhere they seem to melt, seem to give tone to an open area. It can be done by very careful manipulation of the acid, or by grinding down the plate a little.

Goya was a master of the medium; he could play with it. He knew just when to use the tone and what tone, and when to go into etched lines. He was a great master of the medium because he had a point of view on life that interested him so much that the plate and the needle were tools of his expression, not his main concern. He cared more for drawing than the "print."

Lithography

The beauty of lithography is in those rare, tender tones that you get only by drawing on the stone itself. A drawing that is made on paper and transferred to stone is not properly a lithograph, it has none of the qualities of a fine print. The stone has a finer surface than the finest paper in the world. It is like some wonderful crisp silk. When it is surfaced with a fine grain you can get very delicate tones and exquisite lines on it.

Study Daumier's prints. His use of the medium is honest and handsome. He made thousands of lithographs and was able to keep the drawing alive and rich and fresh. Study his, rather than Gavarni's because Daumier's are real drawings. Gavarni could do a lot of things with textures, but his work is apt to slip into sentimentality and cleverness and concern with effects rather than things. It is really best to learn about the use of a medium from those who are master draughtsmen and painters; to learn how to make Things from those who made them well.

Delacroix's illustrations for Goethe's *Faust* are fine prints. The fact that men like Delacroix and Daumier were making illustrations seems to have something to do with the livingness of their prints. They were concerned with something more than making a lithograph. The medium was only incidental and they drew the best qualities out of it for their purposes. Too many making prints nowadays are interested primarily in making prints, they are not interested in life.

It is a good thing to learn about a medium by using subjects that interest you more than the technical process itself. When you have a series of drawings,—butcher shops, subways, bargain basements, parks, and the like, and you feel the need of translating them into another medium, then is a good time to take up lithography or etching. There is no excuse for making prints of concepts that are not worth having around once, let alone a hundred times.

An edition of lithographs, unless it is sold out as an illustration job, is necessarily limited because the artist must pay for the printing at the time of making the stone. With an etching you can put the plate away and print as the edition sells.

Water Color

Water color should be used as a colored drawing rather than a painting medium. Daumier's water colors are first of all drawings, with the color used to make the textures more vital and rich. You don't have to run all over the palette to make a water color. Choose two or three main color relations. Limit your colors as you would in oil painting. Use color sequences, significant changes in color to describe the near and far. Work with lines and color-textures on top of neutral under-tones. Even in the simplest sketch, a few lines and some color washes, there can be separation of form and color.

The trouble with water colors is that you hate to jump into a nice wash to get something more real. Always work on good rag paper so you can clean the wash off with a sponge or bristle brush without destroying the surface of the paper. Cheap paper is so absorbent that the color stains the surface.

With good pigments and fine rag paper, water color is a more permanent medium than oil paint. You can grind your own pigments with gum arabic and a little honey or glycerine as the old painters did, but be sure that the pigment is ground very fine. Pan colors are better to use than tube colors. The latter contain so much glycerine that the paint does not dry properly and the paper may mold because of moisture attracted by the glycerine.

Opaque water color used to touch up a transparent wash drawing is sometimes very useful and necessary to the realization of the thing. (English custom forbids it.) It is well to remember that those opaque tones obliterate the separation of form and color which you have in the transparent washes on white paper.

Pencil, crayon, pastel and pen work well with water color. Use whatever combination of mediums you need, to get realization.

Gouache paintings have a tendency to look like wall paper. But for studying it is an interesting medium. You can melt one tone into another, or lay crisp marks on the dry surface.

When working with gouache you can't let any of the paper show through. The tones dry lighter than when you put them on the paper, which is annoying if you are using a complicated color scheme. Gouache always has a tendency to look like tones with varying tints of white in them. It is very hard to keep air out of the work because of the presence of white in all the pigments. If you put a full dark over a whitened tone the white comes through.

You can use tempera colors instead of gouache. They have more brilliance. If the work is done on a heavy illustration board, you can isolate the tempera and finish the painting with oil glazes.

CHAPTER XII

THE GIST OF IT ALL

ART IS THE RESULT of the creative consciousness of the order of existence. How can there be any ultimate solution of that? Art is the evidence of man's understanding, the evidence of civilization. Humanness is what counts. Man doesn't change much over the centuries, but there is some evidence that he is growing more human, very slowly, although it is his one great reason for being.

The artist has a song to sing. His creative mind is irritated by something he has to say graphically. You don't need to paint masterpieces or monumental subjects. Look out the window. Use your imagination. Get a kick out of that spacial adventure, the textures of things, the reality of the world. Find the design in things.

Seeing frogs and faces in clouds is not imagination. Imagination is the courage to say what you think and not what you see. Max Eastman has said:—The scientist describes water as H_2O; the poet goes further and says "it is wet". We want to describe things that way. **An ideograph** is better than the thing itself. A better work of art tries to say the thing rather than to be the thing. The image has greater realization than the thing itself. That is the great beauty of poetry,—realization brought about by the use of images.

An artist is a product of life, a social creature. Of necessity he cannot mingle with people as much as he would like, but he reaches them through his work. The artist is a spectator of life. He understands it without needing to have physical experiences. He doesn't need to participate in adventures. The artist is interested in life the way God is interested in the universe.

The artist has his own life to live; he has to pause and select and find something to say about it. In his work he seeks to express his understanding with all earnestness. The man of integrity works for himself alone, spurning all temptations to sell out his ability for commercial success. Any artist who paints to suit buyers and critics is what Walter Pach calls an Ananias, and unworthy of the name artist.

We live in a complex world in which we are mutually interdependent. But the artist must be independent. I think he is the only person who has a right to be independent. The artist has always had to fight for his life, for freedom of expression, for the right to say what he believes.

There is no end, no goal in this job of being an artist. The longer you live the further you are from it. An artist may develop very slowly. He may be painting his best picture when he dies at seventy-five. The greatest men like Titian and Rembrandt were always growing, expanding. They didn't reach their top work and then start to repeat. They kept on maturing until they died. A man like Rubens found a great formula and was content to repeat himself. In Rembrandt's later work, done when the public ceased to recognize him, he achieved the greatest plastic realization of all the masters. Old and half blind, he drew with his mind and understanding to please himself, not the public.

The artist is in competition with himself only. A bird does not sing beautifully because there is a contest. Great men are not even aware of competition. Jury exhibitions and the awarding of prizes are detrimental to art. When people vote about matters of taste the thing selected is always mediocre, inoffensive, innocuous.

My life has not been very eventful but my work has made it utterly worthwhile. The only reason I am in the profession is because it is fun. I have always painted for myself and made my living by illustrating and teaching. Some of the etchings and a few paintings made twenty years ago sell now and then, but I have never made a living from my painting. If what I am doing now were selling I would think there was something the matter with it.

It is a sort of escape, a kind of refuge, not to have too much recognition while one is alive. You can go along doing your own work without being bothered too much with what people think. The works live, or rather exist, so much longer than the man.

Selling one's work is the problem of the individual and society. Too much economic success is a bad sign. If you know your history you will know that this is true.

I never thought of one of my good pictures as art while painting it. Whether it was art or not, it was what I wanted to do. Maybe the reason I haven't made a greater position in the history of art is that I am not sufficiently critical of my own work. Like one of those women in the park with a baby, I am proud of it because it is my own, a young hopeful. But we grow more critical in time.

It is better to send pictures to exhibitions and get them fired than to become so self-critical as never to try to exhibit. Anyone who buys the paper to see what the critic is saying about him when he is twenty-five, will take the critic too seriously by the time he is thirty-five.

Young people today are much concerned with having one-man shows. In my day a man didn't expect to have a one-man show until he was about forty-five. It is very bad to be interested in this kind of thing. Too many pictures are being painted for exhibitions with the hope of crashing the museums. The art schools are full of talented students who are carried away by the desire to paint like successful artists, instead of following the line of their own personal desire and interest.

You young people with your fresh minds, must weigh the words of every man over forty-five. I said that when I was forty-five and I am saying it now again. Every time I tell you something, weigh it with your minds. You don't have to take what I say. I am not an authority. There are no authorities over art.

The great artist is the bloom on a plant, which is the art of the period. There may be more than one bloom. All the rest of us are the roots, shoots and branches of that plant or falling petals from the flower. The work we are doing today is a preparation for the great artists who are to come.

We are still individualists. We have no traditional art. There are men like Rivera and Orozco who have been able to assimilate their native racial tradition, but the American Indian art is not close enough to us. We must push along. Perhaps a Naissance is coming here in America. We are working our way toward a healthy art expression. The movement for mural painting has done a great deal to stir the public interest in art, which in turn gives the artist a better chance to live. But for me the most interesting pictures are those that can be put in frames and moved about.

If all art students studied with me and carried on my ideas it would be unfortunate. But I hope that some of the younger artists will get hold of the idea I am working on—this principle of realization. It is the students who spread the idea. In fact, some of the most important teaching is done from student to student.

During the twenty-five years that I have been trying to instruct and inspire others I have learned a great deal from my students. Teaching has made me dig into my own work; I want to say something worthwhile to the fresh young minds with which I come in contact. Because I, too, am a student, ten years ago I turned my back on the type of work I had done in the past, work which had been recognized by critic and public. Many pictures I make today are frankly experiments, products of my laboratory. But in looking over my paintings and etchings of the last ten years, I feel satisfied that a number of them stand out as more powerful and truly creative works than those of my earlier period. Now that I am sixty-eight years old, I am grateful to have lived this long and look forward to more years of hard work. I am just a student, chewing on a bone, the way Picasso is.

GIST OF ART

FORTY YEARS OF PAINTING

A Cross-Section of the Work of John Sloan

A NOTE

THE TASK OF COMMENTING on a collection of pictures like the following could not be left in better hands than those of the artist. The creator's liking for his own work will certainly be excused, and a kindly, fatherly feeling will be readily understood. Unlike the critic, he need not fear that the future will prove him wrong in his judgment. A parent is always right in looking on the better traits of his offspring; and even loving his wayward children.

The present collection is, I think, a fair cross-section of my work for the past forty years. In looking back over the four decades during which I have been painting, I find myself, naturally, more enthusiastic over the efforts of the last ten years. The creative artist will never find many who care to follow in his line of progress. That tiny group which composes the art public, having at first scorned his works of past decades and having finally accepted them, would have him spend his energy in producing more of these now acceptable commodities.

History has proved contemporary estimates to be of little or no value. The painter who has placed his intelligence in command of his actions must always find himself at least a generation ahead of contemporary judgment. And since the artist's own opinion is also a matter of contemporary judgment, the most strictly contemporary of all, I am only asserting his inalienable right to be wrong, a very fundamental human right.

In estimating the works of my past under the light of my ideas of the present, I must acknowledge that they have important qualities. I believed in them then; I believe in them now; just as I thoroughly believe in the importance of my work of the last ten years. In attempting to trace some underlying relationship between my motives past and present, I conclude that the fact that the old pictures of city life were painted from memory furnishes the communicating link. In painting from memory one paints from the thing itself and is not making a visual record. The sense of reality is a mental product which may be carried in the memory and provide all necessary creative impulse. My work of the last ten years has been done with this as a conscious urge, whether done in the presence of the subject matter or from memory.

My present credo is: The eye does not see form but only visual impressions of colors and values. Form is a mental concept deduced from experience. We learn form through the sense of touch. The mind coördinates the memory of tactile sensation with the visual image (color, and light and shade) in apprehending form. The artist, in representing solid form with graphic symbols, must convey the shape with some means apart from color. Color-texture is used as a surface complexion to augment the tangibility of the form.

I believe that this principle—the separation of form and color—could produce thousands of varying results when applied by thousands of different minds.

In providing comments for the pictures in this collection, some selected for excellence, some for variety, some for criticism, I shall endeavor to return to the mood under which they were produced.

J. S.

THE PUBLISHERS are indebted to the various art museums, to the Kraushaar Galleries, and the Grand Central Art Galleries, New York City, and to the private owners mentioned in these pages for the use of photographs of their paintings, and to the Addison Gallery, Andover, Massachusetts, for excerpts from John Sloan's comments on some of the paintings reproduced.

1894—DRAWING, (Philadelphia Inquirer) One of my early newspaper drawings made when I was interested in Japanese prints. I was given recognition as a member of the "poster movement" before I had ever seen the work of Beardsley, Steinlen, Toulouse-Lautrec, and the other European masters of that style. My first efforts as a painter were sketches made on Sunday excursions into the country. I painted for amusement with no idea of making art. Later Henri encouraged me to take up painting seriously.

1901—EAST ENTRANCE, CITY HALL, PHILADELPHIA. In the late 90's a load of hay, a hansom cab, and a Quaker lady were no rare sight in the streets of Philadelphia. A sample of each appears in this painting made when I was still drawing for the 'Philadelphia Press'.

1903—RATHSKELLER, PHILA-
DELPHIA. *To us today, the lady's
costume is quaint, as are the surroundings. But the divided attention
noticeable in the young lady with a
beer escort whose lonely neighbor
is buying champagne, is a symptom
that may be observed today.*

1904—AFTER THE DUEL
DeKock Novels
(Drawing)

1904—BOY WITH PICCOLO.
*One of my earliest canvases. The
influence seems to be the work of
Robert Henri. Color quiet, brushwork fluent. Had I pursued the
course here indicated—but I did not.
There is life in this picture. More
the kind that Hals achieved than
the 'beyond life" of Rembrandt.*

1905—FIFTH AVENUE CRITICS (*Etching*)

1905—CONNOISSEURS OF PRINTS (*Etching*)

1905—THE COFFEE LINE. Winter night, *Fifth Avenue at Madison Square*, and a long line of cold and hungry men waiting their turn for a cup of coffee. This gratuity was a kindly gesture on the part of one of the newspapers. While nothing in its favor, Honorable Mention, Carnegie Institute, 1905, should not be held against it.

1905—SPRING, MADISON SQUARE. The *Flatiron Building and the old Fifth Avenue Hotel* are in the background. An old horse-drawn Fifth Avenue bus with one seat perched back of the driver on the roof, cabs, and long skirts, and a nearby patch of grass with trees. All but the Flatiron Building, things of the past.

1906—FERRY SLIP, WINTER. A non-impressionistic impression of an antique friend of the commuter fighting its way to its berth against the mass of packed ice on a blustery winter afternoon. Painted at the time when New York still awed an unacclimated Pennsylvanian. The tones sombre, handling broad and nervous.

1905—DAISY WITH A DUSTER. A merry-faced Irish girl, who was great fun as a sitter. I remember that I never showed her the finished portrait. I felt that she might not like the imputation of servitude implied by the feather duster.

1906—MOTHER
(*Etching*)

1906—MEMORY
(*Etching*)

1906—DUST STORM. (Collection of the Metropolitan Museum of Art) A dramatic moment on a Sunday afternoon in summer, Fifth Avenue covered by a great gray canopy of cloud, the air full of dust. An early type of automobile chugs up the avenue.

1906—THE PICNIC GROUND. Woods near Bayonne, New Jersey, are the scene in which these adolescent boys and girls frolic like bear cubs. Note the grin that surrounds the gold tooth. Fine grays and whites; easy, active, graphic character of execution.

1906—SUNSET, WEST TWENTY-THIRD STREET. *In the foreground Dolly Sloan, the little woman, looks toward the west from the roof of our studio apartment, not knowing that thirty years later we will have two studios off that way, one in the Hotel Chelsea in the next block, one beyond the horizon in Santa Fe, New Mexico.*

1907—WAKE OF THE FERRY, NO. 1 (Collection of Amelia Elizabeth White) *Another theme perhaps evoked by some nostalgic yearning for Philadelphia. The ferry of course is the first lap of the road home. A melancholy day, when she, to whom the coming landing means nothing, seeks the sad outlook of the vessel's broadening wake. Such was the mood under which this picture was painted. A damage to the canvas within the first few days after its completion led me to paint the subject a second time within a few weeks.*

1906—CHIN ON HAND
(*Drawing*)

1907—PITTSBURGH
(*Drawing*)

1907—WAKE OF THE FERRY, NO. 2. (Collection of the Phillips Memorial Gallery) *This second painting of the theme differs from the first by being in a slightly less melancholy mood. It has been more frequently seen by the public for the reason that the slight repairs to No. 1 were not made for many years.*

1907—MOVIES, FIVE CENTS. *At the time when this picture was painted the cinema was in its sordid infancy, the auditorium a vacant store, admission a nickel. It is interesting to note that the theme of the picture still endures.*

1907—MRS. HENRY REUTER-DAHL. *The wife of the well-known marine painter and illustrator. A charming and clever Icelandic lady who often entertained in their romantic studio home clinging to the cliffs on the brink of the Palisades at Weehawken. A sketch portrait.*

1907—THE HAYMARKET. (*Collection of the Brooklyn Museum*) *This old dance hall on Sixth Avenue, famous through infamy, was a well-known hangout for the underworld. Ladies whose dress and general deportment were satisfactory to the doorman were admitted free. Gents paid.*

1907—HAIR DRESSER'S WINDOW.
*Sixth Avenue had a Coney Island quality
in 1907. It was the Fifth Avenue of the
poor and furnished similar facilities at
lower rates. The process of bleaching the
hair as practised by Mme. Malcomb seems
amusing to the passersby.*

1907—ELECTION NIGHT. *Thirty years
ago the principal spot for the gathering
of the hilarious crowds on Election Night
was Herald Square, Sixth Avenue and 34th
Street. The space was smaller but the
crowds were as thick as those of today.*

1907—SIXTH AVENUE AND THIRTEENTH STREET. This canvas has surely caught the atmosphere of the Tenderloin; drab, shabby, happy, sad, and human. The recent removal of the elevated structure has left it forsaken and dilapidated. Passing through a purgatorial stage.

1907—THROBBING FOUNTAIN, MADISON SQUARE. This circular basin with the jet at water level was a hypnotically attractive feature of old Madison Square. The pulsing spurts were full of rhythmic beauty. No useful purpose was served. Eliminated years ago.

1907—NURSEMAIDS, MADISON SQUARE. A group of young hoydens on an early spring day are very consciously entertaining the men of leisure who occupy the benches. Meanwhile their young charges shift for themselves. Paintings of this period show my resistance of the impressionist influences.

1907—GRAY AND BRASS. (Private Collection) *I well remember how earnest was my intention to bring out the pomp and circumstance that marked the wealthy group in the motor car. The car, gray trimmed with much brass, gave me my title for the picture. This automobile and the veils and dusters are gone today, but the gray lives of the sidewalk are little changed.*

1907—THE COT. (Collection of George Otis Hamlin) *Like all pictures of this period, an extremely limited palette, providing many variants in the whites and grays. The canvas is pervaded with a sense of great peace emanating from a personality. How strange to know that this type of picture was regarded as the work of a "revolutionist in art" by the art criticism of the period in which it was painted.*

1907—PICTURE SHOP WINDOW. (Collection of the Newark Museum) *West Twenty-third Street supplied me with many subjects at this period. I suppose that this unusual interest in pictorial art on the part of the group here shown gave the painter hope for the future of art in America.*

1907—DOLLY WITH BLACK BOW. *It has always seemed to me that one's own family are the painter's most difficult sitters. It is perhaps because his mind is divided between the creative and the critical. He may fail to satisfy himself in both directions.*

1907—KENT CRANE. *Son of an artist—perhaps this accounts for the alert eyes and quizzical mouth. Gold blond hair, ruddy face and a white tie break the gray tones. Vigorously stated.*

1908—WILLIAM S. WALSH. "Billy" Walsh was for several years literary editor of the New York Herald. A burly man with a mind of the first order, a fountain of information. His book, a bulky Dictionary of Literary Curiosities, contained only a small part of the mass of oddities and out-of-the-way data he had collected. New York's bohemians loved him.

1908—SOUTH BEACH BATHERS. This Staten Island resort had few visitors compared to Coney Island, and gave better opportunity for observation of individual behavior. It is amusing to recall how very chic the bathing costume of the girl standing seemed at the time.

1909—SAVINGS BANK
(Drawing)

1908—HUDSON SKY. (Collection of the Wichita Art Museum) Two or three weeks at M. Richard's 'pension', Coytesville on the Palisades, was a first opportunity for a continuous series of landscapes of which this may be the most important. A strangely beautiful cloud formation that hung for hours like a giant white dome overhead. The clear line of blue between the clouds ran straight across the zenith from horizon to horizon.

1909—RECRUITING, UNION SQUARE. A peacetime recruiting sergeant and a possible customer. Union Square in those days had not been undermined by the subways and in summer a fountain, the flowers, and the trees made it a cool and shady haven for the unemployed, qualities claimed for the army.

1909—THREE A. M. Night vigils at the back window of a Twenty-third Street studio were rewarded by motifs of this sort; many of them were used in my etchings. Some of the lives that I glimpsed I thought I understood. These two girls I took to be sisters, one of whom was engaged in some occupation that brought her home about this hour of the morning. On her arrival the other rose from her slumbers and prepared a meal. This picture is redolent with the atmosphere of a poor, back, gaslit room. It has beauty, I'll not deny it; it must be that human life is beautiful.

1909—FIFTH AVENUE. (Collection of John F. Kraushaar) *An impression of the Avenue walking south from Thirty-fifth Street. Perhaps nobody but I will recognize the old Waldorf on the right but the Flatiron Building at Twenty-third Street will be clear to anybody. I have been told that the lady in black with the rose was undoubtedly Katharine Clemens Gould.*

1909—CHINESE RESTAURANT. *On Sixth Avenue, in this New York in which I still preferred to feel a stranger. The girl is feeding her boy friend, before taking him home, in one of the many Chinese restaurants of that day where only Chinese food was served. Graphic expression and resonant in color.*

1910—PIGEONS. (Collection of the Boston Museum of Fine Arts) Whether these pigeon fanciers earned a living by the sale of squabs or the sale of votes was never quite sure in my mind. In the background across the roofs of the Tenderloin district is seen the Pennsylvania Railroad terminal, then under construction.

1909—CLOWN MAKING UP. (Collection of the Phillips Memorial Gallery) Truth to tell this picture was painted under the inspiration of an enthusiastic model with a clown suit. One of my first results using the Maratta palette. Precise and easy in execution—well controlled light.

1910—SCRUBWOMEN IN
THE OLD ASTOR LIBRARY.
(Collection of Mrs. Cyrus Mc-
Cormick) *These jolly strong-arm
women in the golden brown and
musty surroundings of thousands
of books aroused a strong urge to
fix them on canvas. The result
was and is very satisfactory to the
painter. This has become a historical record, as any picture of
contemporary life is sure to be.*

1910—THE COBURN PLAYERS. *This is an impression of a beautiful occasion,
an outdoor performance on the campus of Columbia University. Many details are
omitted—among them I note the absence of the mosquitos. These small pests
attended to our ankles while the Coburns kept our minds amused.*

1909—GIRL IN FUR HAT. This must be a good one for it was hung in a National Academy Exhibition in 1909, the last year that I offered work to that honorable jury. There is clear light and substance to this portrait which I hope justifies my liking for it.

1910—YOLAND IN LARGE HAT. I believe this is what is called a dated picture although I am not sure whether it was painted in 1910 or 1909. The same Yoland in hat, feather, and big bow of the period.

1910—YOLAND IN GRAY TIP-
PET. (Private Collection) *An elfin
personality was Yoland and this
picture gives that quality. Gray violet hat and jacket, gray and white
notes of muff and tippet are the
color theme. A lovable picture for
many people—myself included.*

1910—YOLAND SINGING. *One
of the several canvases devoted to
the attempt to catch and fix some
of the lovely fire and spirit of this
young girl. She worked hard and
liked to pose, and yet she flitted
about like a bird.*

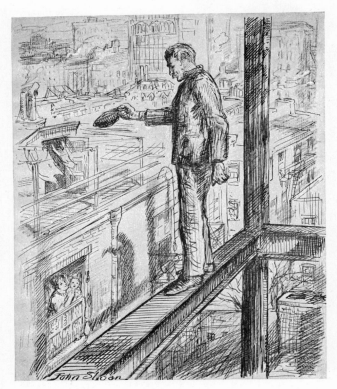

1911—SALUTE
(*Drawing*)

1911—PICTURE BUYER
(*Etching*)

1910—YEATS AT PETITPAS'. (Collection of the Corcoran Gallery)
Petitpas', pension and restaurant, is still located on West Twenty-ninth Street,
although the three charming sisters who ran it have since returned to France.
At the time the picture was painted the great human drawing card of Petitpas'
was John Butler Yeats, the charming Irish conversationalist, artist, and phil-
osopher, father of W. B. Yeats, the Irish poet. Yeats' table drew young poets,
painters, writers, and actors who eagerly enjoyed his talk which was always
greatly entertaining. In the painting from left to right—Van Wyck Brooks,
J. B. Yeats, Alan Seeger, who wrote 'Rendezvous with Death', Dolly Sloan,
Ann Squire, John Sloan, Fred King. It is a satisfaction to have painted this
record of Yeats whose portraits in Dublin and England establish him, ac-
cording to Robert Henri, as the best British portrait painter of the Victorian
era. He died in New York at the age of eighty-four.

1911—ISADORA DUNCAN. No painting that I could possibly produce could express my adoration for Isadora. This attempt made soon after first seeing her marvelous dancing goes to prove it, I fear. My excuse must be that I viewed her through a mist of unshed tears. She lifted human movement to the level of the divine. We ne'er shall look upon her like again.

1911—SAVINGS BANK. The odor of the sanctity of money was my literary motive behind the painting of this interior of the Greenwich Savings Bank on lower Sixth Avenue. I like the picture and feel that the preaching is not too obvious. What was the first cause has become of little importance in the result.

1911—WOMAN'S WORK. *In color this painting is noticeable for a quiet but out of the ordinary quality. Painted with a set palette of adjusted tones. The subject, a woman putting out her wash, is one that never loses its charm for me.*

1911—TAMMANY HALL. *It is good to have something left by which to remember this painting of the old wigwam on Fourteenth Street. The building lasted longer than the picture, which was lost in a transportation accident.*

1912—A WINDOW ON THE STREET. (Collection of George Otis Hamlin)
The color theme of this canvas is, I think, in close harmony with the subject.
The sullen wistfulness of the woman whose housekeeping was limited to one
room. Dominant red purple cushion and smothered red brickwork.

1912—CARMINE THEATER. Wistful little customers hanging around a small
movie show. In those days it was called "ash can art"—today it's the "American Scene".

1912—SPRING, GRAMERCY PARK. A very direct and colorful impression of a precious spot in New York. This unique privately controlled park excludes all but certified residents of the neighborhood. Snobbish but beautiful.

1912—McSORLEY'S BAR. (Collection of the Detroit Museum of Art) The "Old House at Home" as it was called was, and still is, located on East Seventh Street near Cooper Union. A favorite out of the way retreat for appreciative ale drinkers. Behind its dust covered front window, an ancient bar, sawdust covered floor, walls crowded with old theatrical and sporting prints and programmes. It survived almost alone the modernizing of the saloon. This painting was the first of several painted of McSorley's and has been much appreciated during the years since prohibition was repealed.

1912—SIX O'CLOCK, WINTER. (Collection of the Phillips Memorial Gallery) *The Third Avenue elevated structure near Eighteenth Street. The last rays of the winter sun affect only the sky. From 1909 on I planned and mixed all colors on the palette before starting each picture. No color scheme was repeated.*

1912—SPRING RAIN. (Collection of the Whitney Museum of American Art) *Memory tells me that my motive was to record this glimpse of an ankle (an ankle counted in those days) and the fresh green and the spring rain. I think however, that what endures is the special chord of color to which I set my palette. Graphic interest sustains this and subject matter is of minor importance.*

1912—SUNDAY IN UNION SQUARE. (Collection of George Otis Hamlin)
Few paintings are very satisfactory to the artist at the time of making. How glad we are years after that we tried our best—building better than we knew. Lavender light was in my mind.

1912—SUNDAY, GIRLS DRYING THEIR HAIR. (Collection of the Addison Gallery)
Another of the human comedies which were regularly staged for my enjoyment by the humble roof-top players of Cornelia Street.

1913—PICTURE HAT (Drawing)

1913—THE NET RESULT
The Masses (Drawing)

1912—BLOND NUDE. (Collection of George Otis Hamlin) Shown in the first Independent Exhibition, 1917. Forceful painting—harmed by perspective observed in small far arm.

1912—McSORLEY'S BACK
ROOM. (Collection of Miss Julia
Peck) *McSorley's back room was
like a sacristy. Here old John Mc-
Sorley would sit greeting old friends
and philosophizing. Women were
never served, indeed the dingy walls
and woodwork looked as if women
had set neither hand nor foot in the
place. Painted from pencil sketch.*

1913—SKETCH PORTRAIT. *At
least so it seems today. It may have
had more important motives at the
time it was painted. Dashing brushwork—not important today. Good
color. But a rather visual concept.*

1913—EVE AND ADAM—STROLLING
The Masses (Drawing)

1913—ROSETTE. (Collection of George Otis Hamlin) The name was suggested by Theophile Gautier's 'Mlle. de Maupin'. The picture is a charming, easily painted study in lavender, grays, and tonal whites. The flesh tones delicate and yet of sufficient substance.

1912—RENGANESCHI'S SATURDAY NIGHT. (Collection of the Art Institute of Chicago) Renganeschi, Restaurante de la Republica de San Marino, the oldest republic in the world, bounded on all sides by Italy. A water color drawing on the wall was a full length and breadth portrait of the native land of which he was so proud. These matters all explained by Signor Renganeschi in person to all interested. Renganeschi's was and still is, I believe, located on West Tenth Street, a stone's throw from Jefferson Market jail. The quality of light and sense of the place, as well as the life of the dining room—quite satisfactory.

1914—PLAYING TO
EMPTY SEATS
Harper's Weekly
(Drawing)

1913—SPRING PLANTING.
(Collection of W. B. Maxwell) *In
1912-1913 our living quarters on
West Fourth Street overlooked
Greenwich Village back yards. The
picture fixes a lovely spring day and
a group of merry boarders in the
next door yard fired with momen-
tary energy to till the soil.*

1913—ITALIAN CHURCH PROCESSION.
(Collection of the Fine Arts Gallery, San
Diego) *Properly dated 1913 although very
important finishing matters were not painted
until 1925. These religious festivals in the
Italian quarters of New York were and still
are colorful invasions of very drab localities.
Wooden squared arches span the streets draped
with bright bunting and electric lights fes-
tooned overhead. I remember the palette as
a violet dominant.*

1914—"LUDLOW, COLORADO, 1914"
The Masses
(Drawing)

[239]

1915—ISADORA DUNCAN
The Masses
(Drawing)

1914—WHITE HOUSE AND
SUMACS. *My first summer in Gloucester afforded the first opportunity for
continuous work in landscape, and I
really made the most of it. Working
from nature gives, I believe, the best
means of advance in color and spontaneous design.*

1914—BACK YARDS,
GREENWICH VILLAGE.
(Collection of the Whitney
Museum of American Art)
*During the period when I oc-
cupied the studio in the loft
building on Sixth Avenue, my
wife and I lived in a small
apartment in the neighborhood overlooking these yards.
This picture was painted from
memory after careful observation of material. The winter atmosphere and color well rendered, the cats unforgettable.*

1915—BACHELOR GIRL
    (Drawing)

1915—SALLY, STRIPED DRESS.
Sally Stanton from next door, liked
all the pictures I painted of her.
Always a willing model full of the
wiry energy of twelve years. We
were great chums. I learned lots
about painting working from her.

1915—FROG POND. What we
called the moors lying between bay
and ocean were rich in material.
This fresh water pond was an inspiration for lush color and light.

1914—LOVE ON THE ROOF
(Etching)

1914—THE RED PAINT MILL. On Rocky Neck this old factory made marine paints for ship builders. There were no makers of artists' oil colors although picture making was a chief industry in Gloucester in the summer.

1915—ROCKS AND SEA. One of the
many small pictures painted on the
back shore. The long walk from East
Gloucester laden with canvases, easel,
and paintbox was splendid exercise.
When we came home we were bodily
tired. Sometimes spiritually, too.

1915—SUN AND WIND ON THE
ROOF. (Collection of Charles
Whalen) An urge to record my strong
emotional response to the city woman,
any woman running up the colors of
a fresh clean wash. Sun, wind, scant
clothing, blowing hair, unconscious
grace give me great joy. This is a try
at handing it on.

1915—SALLY, SARAH AND
SADIE, PETER AND PAUL. *All
the parts in this gymnastic comedy
were played for my entertainment
by Sally, her cats, and the old apple
tree. I think it's a fine rollicking
piece of picture making. Drawing
with paint.*

1916—GLOUCESTER HARBOR.
*Painted from Gloucester's tallest
building at that time. I think it
was four stories high. The painting
itself is not before me, but my
memory of it is agreeable. A very
clear memory of neutraled crimsons
and blues and warm grays.*

**1916—SIGNORINA CHERU-
BINO.** (Collection of the Whitney
Museum of American Art) *Posed
by Amelia Rose. A direct piece of
painting of this period. Not as sculptural as I might wish to get it were
I painting it today. I seldom get my
wish, anyway. Fine color quality.*

1915—WIND ON THE BAY.
(Collection of George Otis Hamlin)
*A freshly painted and spontaneous
picture of Gloucester Harbor. I feel
that the foreground is a little over-
dominating in the composition. With
the owner's permission I might some
time cut it down.*

1916—HORACE TRAUBEL. *This portrait gives me an opportunity to write a friend's admiring tribute to a great American who was content to live in the shadow of Walt Whitman. His "With Walt Whitman in Camden" out-Boswells Boswell in detail of the years he waited on Walt hand and foot and brain. The files of his periodical—"The Conservator" prove him to be a thinker and poet in his own right.*

1916—EVENING, ROCKY NECK. *A mere handful of the people of East Gloucester lived on Rocky Neck but in summer the artist colony was quite numerous. Such a fishing village atmosphere as is shown in this picture creates a longing to see it all again. But it is probably all messed up with automobiles in various stages of decay, exhaust odors fighting the fishy ones.*

1916—PLAY ON THE ROCKS. *Posing for the artist, if it could be called posing, was something these Gloucester children seemed to thoroughly enjoy, and I know that the artist was happy working with them. Most appreciative critics they were, so easily pleased, so understanding.*

1917—DOLLY BY THE KITCHEN DOOR. *Five or six happy summers were spent in Gloucester. Each year we moved into our little red and white cottage and each day was passed in painting the dunes, the sky, the rocks, the bay, and sea. This picture of homely interest is handsomely forthright in color.*

1916—HILL, MAIN STREET, GLOUCESTER. Down this picturesque dip
into town rolls a blue Mercedes, a few years old but full of pep and power.
The driver is Randall Davey who painted in Gloucester several summers. The
picture is rich in tone and was painted on the spot.

1916—SIGNALS. (Collection of George Otis Hamlin) A warship in the harbor
with all her bunting displayed, and a wash gaily flapping in reply from a line
on the shore are back of the title of this picture which speaks pretty well for
itself even in black and white.

1917—RED ROCKS AND QUIET SEA. *I have a distinct memory of that long, straight edge of the ocean at the horizon. The sea so quiet that it seemed like a great blue wall. The red granite rocks were at a slant and sharp and tiring to the feet. Plenty of patient persistence on the painter's part.*

1916—THE TOWN STEPS, GLOU-CESTER. (Collection of the Harrison Gallery, Los Angeles Museum) *Thoroughly satisfactory is my memory of this painting refreshed by the photograph. These wooden steps were a pedestrian thoroughfare connecting streets on two levels. The girls are healthy types of the native population. Rich in color and convincing in light. I'd like to see it again.*

1917—REDDY IN THE TREE.
A happy little boy from Gloucester
town, who was glad to earn a little
money by sitting for the "attist".
Several studies record his sun-pink
face and carrotty hair. He was a
friendly, likable, little fellow who
said he thought he would be tough
like his brother in about a year!

**1917—MAIN STREET, GLOU-
CESTER.** An example of small
town life from Gloucester. This picture was painted on the spot with
my easel set up in the main street.
Apart from the unpleasantness of
an encounter with an intoxicated
man whose inquiry, "What d'yer
think yer doin'?" was a bit discon-
certing, I had no trouble with the
audience, but I made no more attempts in that fisherman's town to
paint life from the street.

1917—GRACE EMERSON, DANCER. *I like this picture. It seems to me a very honest piece of painting. How earnestly this girl worked trying to help me catch this movement which was part of a beautiful sequence. While not true in this case, the model often works harder than the painter.*

1917—GLOUCESTER TROLLEY. *This, too, is history. The trolleys from Rocky Neck are gone now, busses have replaced them. No doubt the same summer visitor type of crowd fill the busses. But the little woman and Reddy in the foreground went to town long ago.*

1917—MY WIFE IN BLUE. (Collection of Amelia Elizabeth White) *My hardest working model. In our little parlor in the red house in Gloucester she sat without a rest for five hours in the first pose for this portrait. I am never quite satisfied with the "likeness" when I paint her. This is a good portrait and a good piece of painting. Who's going to say it here if I do not?*

1917—YOUNG GIRL READING.
Here is a case of visual perspective
exaggerating the length of legs. This
was partly due to the tiny room in
which I worked. So close was I to
the sofa that I recorded what I saw
and had not room to back away to
see what I painted. Conscious resistance of perspective distortion was
what I needed, not more room.
Sturdily painted, good color, rich,
well planned.

1917—FLATS AT LOW TIDE.
(Collection of George Otis Hamlin)
The mud flats running out to Rocky
Neck were the clam diggers' op-
portunity at low tide. Artists were
plugging away at their work in the
studios shown and many others.
Every man to his trade.

1918—BLEECKER STREET SATURDAY NIGHT. *This old thoroughfare in the Greenwich Village section was once a fashionable residence street. It has maintained a great deal of the old architecture. On Saturday nights the small shops and sidewalk merchants do a lively business. The amputated building shown had been recently curtailed in cutting through the new 7th Ave. downtown. A cheerful, happy street, there's many another bleaker.*

1917—GERTRUDE S. DRICK, "WOE" (Private Collection) *Her visiting card was edged in heavy black and bore the single word "woe". When asked to explain, her reply was simply, "Woe is me." She had a witty, quick intelligence and I believe she liked to do the unexpected, especially during the years she lived in Greenwich Village. A happy memory—here's luck to her.*

1918—BLOND NUDE, ROSE
SCARF. *This is a beautiful canvas.
The tonal relations are fine. If
designing the figure today I would
use more foreshortening in the
legs. Other times, other manners.*

1918—ROCKS AND WIL-
LOWS. *This is a full landscape,
very satisfactory to its author. A
few steps from the little red house
where we lived, the old rock forma-
ations with trees and bushes afforded great opportunities for study.*

1918—"I MUST BE ABOUT MY FATHER'S BUSINESS". *My only picture with religious subject matter. Made to order for an exhibition of "Childhood of Christ" pictures arranged by Mrs. Sterner. Not a "typical Sloan"—I hope that the pictures in the collection will prove that there is no such thing. Plague on the classifiers anyway!*

1918—EFZENKA, THE CZECH. *(Collection of Mrs. Cyrus McCormick) This queer looking name is Eugenia to us. One of the Stein sisters, well liked models for twenty years. Robert Henri painted Stein many times, some of his most important canvases resulted. She had strong opinions on politics and society and her English was odd but understandable. Good model and friend. Where now?*

1918—THE COW. (Collection
of the Phillips Memorial Gallery)
*Cows and artists were not en-
couraged to associate in Gloucester. I did not paint them often,
perhaps for that reason. Artists
sometimes left paint rags behind them and the cows who
had a taste for that kind of thing
were made quite ill.*

1919—OLD PORTALE,
SANTA FE. *The last survival of
the roofed sidewalks which once
gave Santa Fe a thoroughly
foreign appearance, Coy maids
and mashers have not been
abolished.*

1918—THE RED LANE. A quiet wagon road, muddy and red, between willows beside a pond in East Gloucester. Directly painted. The composition quite natural. This picture is one of the lost or strayed, or—Whereabouts unknown.

1919—HOTEL DANCE IN SANTA FE. Our contemporary life soon becomes history. This festive gathering at the old De Vargas hotel in the large, high-ceilinged dining room draped with flags covering the windows, is an echo of the past. The old hotel went up in flames years ago. The dances also have gone up in price and social pretense.

1919—KOSHARE. (Collection of Dr. Edgar L. Hewett) *A preliminary of the Corn Dance at Santo Domingo is the reenactment of an ancient ceremony in which the ancestral spirits consult on the coming dance, scouting the points of the compass for enemies. Assured on this point the Koshare proceed slowly through the Plaza and return to the kiva and the dancers come forth for the ceremony.*

1920—THE PLAZA, EVENING, SANTA FE. (Collection of Mrs. Cyrus McCormick) *This promenade is a regular feature of the nights when the Santa Fe band plays on the Plaza during the summer. Our own family party is at the left.*

1920—CORPUS CHRISTI, SANTA FE. *A group of girls from the church orphanage passing a temporary altar by the side of Camino Delgado in the annual procession early in June.*

1919—STREET IN MOON-LIGHT, SANTA FE. *Camino San Francisco, once the western road out of town, has preserved much of its appearance of a hundred years ago. A view of the old street in clear moonlight.*

1920—ROMANY MARYE.
Greenwich Village's famous
hostess, philosopher, and friend.
This portrait like most such painted first for the painter, only just
got by with the sitter. The anima-
tion and dynamic personality of
Marye would baffle a better por-
traitist than I.

1920—TWELVE APOSTLES.
Eroded sandstone formations on
Little Tesuque Creek, named by
this painter. This canyon, which
has now been set aside as a park,
is rich in fossils proving that what
is now eight thousand feet above
sea level was once beneath the sea.

1920—PICNIC ON THE RIDGE. (Private Collection) Mahonri Young, the Biesels, the Shusters, Myra Thomas, Martha Simpson, Lois Wright, Mae Larsen, O. Wells, two pups, many hot dogs, and an old gray Ford, a couple of miles out on the North Road.

1919—THE EAGLE DANCE. (Collection of Frank C. Osborn) An unforgettable ceremonial which displays at its best the Indian's deep harmony with all nature. Simple, unimitative, but profound. This performance is by the Eagles of Tesuque.

1921—SUNLIT PEAK, SANTA FE CANYON. *The reservoir in the foreground is a source of Santa Fe's water supply. Randall Davey's ranch is just around the bend.*

1921—TWO SENORAS, SANTA FE. *In 1921 black shawled matrons were not so rare as they are today. The combination of the historic black shawls with short skirts seemed to me curious enough to be recorded. Twin hills in the distance to match.*

1921—EAGLES OF TESUQUE.
Within nine miles of a European-
ized city, for three hundred years
the little Pueblo of Tesuque has
made a noble fight against combined poverty and civilization. The
population is small and on the day
when we saw this ceremony a mere
handful appeared as spectators.

1921—HOMBRES IN THE
GARDEN. Our orchard garden in
Santa Fe, with Georgio Valdes,
faithful servitor of the old school,
turning up the soil in spring. Each
year his spade uncovered old shards
of Indian pottery, common china-
ware, Civil War uniform buttons,
old cartridges. A skull was unearth-
ed one day while we dug a well.

1922—COYOTE MESA. (Collection of George Otis Hamlin) *A painting must have a name. I took the liberty of naming this mesa which is on the edge of the Carson National Forest in New Mexico. As I stood there, painting, I heard a purring sound behind me—the next moment I was engaged in a battle with a twister that carried my hat a hundred yards away and spilled my equipment.*

1922—OLD JEMEZ MISSION. *Ruin of the ancient mission church in the extinct Jemez Pueblo. Note the proud Ford owner snapshooting his family on this almost prehistoric spot.*

1922—THE CITY FROM GREENWICH VILLAGE. Looking south over lower Sixth Avenue from the roof of my Washington Place studio, on a winter evening. The distant lights of the great office buildings downtown are seen in the gathering darkness. The triangular loft building on the right had contained my studio for three years before. Although painted from memory it seems thoroughly convincing in its handling of light and space. The spot on which the spectator stands is now an imaginary point since all the buildings as far as the turn of the elevated have been removed, and Sixth Avenue has been extended straight down to the business district. The picture makes a record of the beauty of the older city which is giving way to the chopped-out towers of the modern New York. Pencil sketch provided details.

1920—MOTHER AND DAUGHTER. Twenty years ago this contrast in costume between mother and daughter was more frequently seen in the ancient city than it is today. Middle-aged women are now less sedate, more up to date.

1922—CHURCH OF THE PENITENTES, CHIMAYO, N. M. (Collection of the Newark Museum.) The Penitentes is a secret religious organization that dates far back in the history of New Mexico. The weird procession of flagellants bearing the cross and chanting mournfully in the night is a sight that is seldom seen by visitors.

1922—DANCE AT COCHITI PUEBLO, NEW MEXICO. This ceremonial Corn Dance of the Cochiti Indians brings a large crowd to the Pueblo. The horsemen on the right are visiting Navajos.

1922—BURROS THRESHING. A memory of my first sight of this really exciting survival of old times. It would seem more practical to employ the old wooden flail, but the gente seem to prefer to flail the recalcitrant burros.

1923—GROTESQUES AT SANTO DOMINGO. *I think I am in a position to inform the reader that the grotesques in the picture are in the immediate foreground. The word could not be well applied to the Koshare whose actions and chant and dress make them more than humanly natural. They truly seem of the ancient world.*

1922—EL GALLO, SANTO DOMINGO PUEBLO. *An equestrian game of Spanish origin, a great favorite with the Pueblo horsemen. A chicken strung between two poles is "it".*

1922—JEFFERSON MARKET, SIXTH AVENUE. *From 1914 to 1927 my studio on Washington Place at Sixth Avenue provided this view to the north, with the old Jefferson Market overlooking the Sixth Avenue elevated. The jail and market have since been torn down, giving place to a huge jail structure. The painting might be called a study in red and red-orange, and was painted from my studio window.*

1923—SISTERS AT THE
WINDOW
(Etching)

1923—RESTING, STRIPED
BLANKET. One reason I include
this picture is because of the resistance of perspective between the near
and far arms. Directly painted with
evident color-sculptural motives.

1922—FIGURES IN THE DANCE. These boys of Ildefonso Pueblo followed by their wives are selected as the motif typical of the Corn Dance at San Ildefonso. Note the mesa, upper right, the top formation like a great sarcophagus supporting the clouds.

1924—NUDE SEATED looking back (Drawing)

1924—SPRING FLOWERS. *This picture has, in a very direct, simple way, handed on the thrill that comes to everyone on a wet spring morning from the first sight of the flower huckster's wagon. The brilliant notes of the plants surrounded on all sides by wet, city grays. Dolly at the left.*

1924—THRESHING FLOOR, SANTA FE. *Within the limits of the ancient city until recently, this primitive process could be seen each autumn. A herd of goats was driven in circular stampede around a level floor of sunbaked mud.*

1924—TRAVELLING CARNIVAL.
These collapsible and portable enter-
tainments, when permitted by the city
authorities to flaunt their charms are
a tremendous success with the people.
Indians, Spanish, and Anglos—as we
are called—enjoy the agreeable change
from the flickering films.

1924—EDGAR VARÈSE, COM-
POSER. Talking with Varèse while
working on this picture was a musical
education wasted on me. His hope
for an invention which would electri-
cally produce thousands of tonal vibrations exactly as planned by the com-
poser, was the cause for the contrap-
tions in the background.

1924—DANCERS IN THE DUST. (Collection of Mrs. Spencer Browne) Corn
Dance, Santo Domingo, enveloped in a swirl of dust. Eyes, mouths, and ears
filled with the gritty particles, but the show must go on.

1924—WEST WASHINGTON SQUARE, EVENING. (Collection of Oliver
B. James) This child left the studio where it was born for a better home in a
very short time. It is a city picture with great charm. The arc lights fresh lit,
the children on skates darting about like clattering night birds.

1924—GRAND CENTRAL STATION. The warm gray interior of the great station. A sense of vast space, stabbed by two shafts of afternoon sun. I hope that the attempt to establish a kind of order in a scattered crowd has been successful.

1924—A ROAD TO SANTA FE. (Collection of Edward S. Rosenthal) From the North Road we see Santa Fe, the Cerrillos Mountains, and the great Sandia (Watermelon) Mountain, southern boundary of the Tewa world.

1925—DOLLY WITH MANTIL-
LA. This portrait of "herself" was
painted in Santa Fe. The likeness
in this case is rather satisfactory and
I remember that the canvas was
completed quite rapidly. We "Anglos" go in for Spanish mantillas in
Santa Fe. The natives too often
choose their styles from the mail-
order catalogues.

1925—SCULPTURE IN THE
SQUARE
(*Etching*)

1925—SNOWSTORM IN THE VILLAGE
(*Etching*)

1925—EVE OF SAINT FRANCIS, SANTA FE. *The official name of the old city is Ciudad Real de Santa Fe de San Francisco. The eve of the patron saint's day is marked by a beautiful night procession leaving the cathedral in the background.*

1926—RECLINING FIGURE
(Drawing)

1925—VICTORIA. Miss Ebbels,
she was then, a former student
of mine. Since that time she has
made herself a place as artist
lithographer. A careful canvas
harmonious in tone.

1925—TWO SISTERS. A case of double exposure or dual personality or second sight. A double attempt at a portrait of a single Santa Fe girl—Alejandra Rael, Aleck for short, since married. A handsome Spanish-American type. Composed right well —the picture, I mean.

1926—NUDE STANDING
BY TABLE
(Drawing)

1926—NUDE *head back,*
legs foreshortened
(Drawing)

1926—NUDE, Red and Green (Drawing)

1926—FASHIONS OF THE PAST
line and aquatint
(Etching)

1926—NUDE *Green and Brown*
(Drawing)

1926—EASTER EVE
line and aquatint
(Etching)

1926-LITTLE RANCH HOUSE.
An expanse of grooved gravel and soil stretching off toward the Rio Grande. The little native casita whose owner, when not working in the fields, is found seated on the shady side in summer, on the sunny side in winter.

1926—THE WHITE WAY. A sudden impulse to paint Broadway with its lights in a snowfall took me to Broadway and Fifty-third Street on this cold winter night. There I stood with pencil clutched in petrified fingers, making memoranda which resulted in this painting. The realization of my surroundings had been frozen in my memory, but I feel that my suffering has been compensated for.

1926—WATER AND LIGHT, SANTA FE. Some years ago the power and light for Santa Fe were home made, now wires bring the current from dynamos nearer the coal supply. In the old days, warm sprays from the condensers filled a pool where the boys of the town had great fun. Water is a precious thing in New Mexico.

1926—BATHERS IN THE
ACEQUIA. (Collection of Gertrude
Strain) *A cool swiftly flowing irriga-*
tion ditch carrying precious water to
the arid country north of Santa Fe.
A hot day—so called—but at seven
thousand feet above sea level we do
not really know what heat is. Two
artists' wives take to the water like
improved ducks. Memory brought
back the scene.

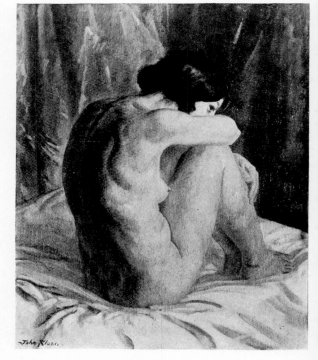

1926—NUDE GLANCING
BACK. *Well painted and well de-*
signed and the sense of surface reali-
zation is quite thorough. The glance
of the single eye from under the
dark hair is an amusing incident.

1926—CHIMAYO COUNTRY.
Horses fording the river west of
Chimayo during a dry spell. These
trickling streams become raging tor-
rents immediately after a heavy rain.

1927—PRACTICAL MUFFS
(Drawing)

1927—CHAMA RUNNING RED. The river is running like pink tomato soup down to the Rio Grande and the Gulf of Mexico, carrying off the good red earth.

1927—THE PLAZA, NOON. The Plaza Santa Fe was planned by the King of Spain before the landing of our Pilgrim Fathers. It has had periods of sun and shade, according to the amount of attention paid the trees. This picture was made during the supervision of the Women's Board of Trade.

1927— BUSSES IN THE SQUARE. On summer afternoons and holidays long
lines of waiting customers piled onto the roof of each departing bus. This
picture depicts a day in spring with the new leaves of the trees in the park
new-born into a dusty world.

1927—NUDE LOOKING OUT WINDOW. The golden red hair with side buns is character-
istically a Carmen style. She was a very popular model with painters and sculptors. Beautiful,
ruddy complexion and a friendly personality, with great interest in the work.

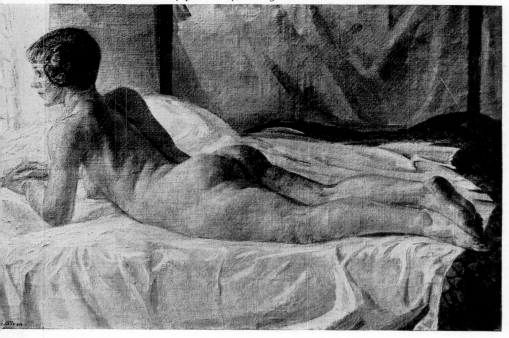

1927—ROAD TO CIENEGA. (Collection of George Otis Hamlin) *An old side road to the little, gold-bearing hills of Cerillos. The vivid green of a tree evidences a stream in an otherwise arid country. It looks like a lettuce in New York.*

1928—SIXTH AVENUE AND THIRD STREET. (Collection of the Whitney Museum of American Art) *I have always been interested in the el trains with their flashing lights. It seems to me that there is more of a sense of realization in this painting than in earlier works of a similar nature. An increase in color-plastic strength.*

1927—LAFAYETTE HOTEL. (Collection of the Metropolitan Museum of Art) *This old hostelry on University Place has always been famous for the fine quality of its cuisine. It has also been a favorite resort of literary and artistic personages. To the passerby not looking for the modern glitter, it has always had a look of cheer and comfort, particularly on a wet evening such as this. I will admit that in painting its exterior I chose the aspect most familiar to me. The picture seems to me to be a successful example of chiaroscuro. Color and form are separate and simultaneous.*

1928—THE WIGWAM (*Etching*)

1928—WET NIGHT WASHING-
TON SQUARE. (Collection of
Philip B. Goetz) This little picture
met such swift appreciation that I
hardly owned it long enough to
make its acquaintance. It is pleasant
to see it again though only in reproduction. My memory recalls the
success of the night-lighted showery
plaza with busses and cars.

1928—LARGE WHITE NUDE.
I believe this to be a rather successful effort—the world is full of them.
Painting the Irish milk-white body
complexion, a whiteness that occurs,
so far as I know, in no other race,
places many difficulties in the way
of exact color sculpture. It is one of
the larger canvases. Incidentally, the
projecting hand would be helped by
more of the foreshortening which
has been used in the arm.

1928—McSORLEY'S AT HOME. A group of old timers at a table in the front of the "Old House at Home". While Ed, the pot-boy, was sometimes within call, most customers waited on themselves. The five-toed cat, (count 'em if you can) is paying attention to a German-American who was a regular until 1917 when we went into the war to end war. After that he faded out of the picture. But I held him in my memory.

1927—SUNMOUNT ARROYO. Erosion coming to town. Now happily stopped along with thousands of others by the boys of the C. C. C.

1928—NUDE WITH BOOK-
LET. (Collection of the Whitney Museum of American Art)
A very fine nude whose quality
is attested by the present
ownership. The glittering, fiery
orange drapery across the far
edge of the couch is a very
striking element. Direct in
painting and successful in its
tangibility of surface.

1928—ANN IN COSTUME.
Dressed for a costume party,
Ann Brockman's little hat was
old fashioned then, now it is
quite the latest thing. This
portrait was underpainted in
monochrome with lead white in
oil, glazed two days later with
thin varnish oil tones. It is in
perfect condition now, although
some drier was used in the first
painting. One of my first paintings made with technical
separation of form and color.

[294]

1929—CHARCOAL FIGURE
(Drawing)

1928—SPRING, WASHINGTON SQUARE. *For eight years my studio overlooked Washington Square. As is so often the case, the fact that it was always there ready and waiting seemed to prevent my using it as often as I should have done. This picture may be of special interest because it represents a transition between direct painting and the "mixed technique". It was started in pale, neutral tones and then worked up with more positive colors—with some glazing in the final work.*

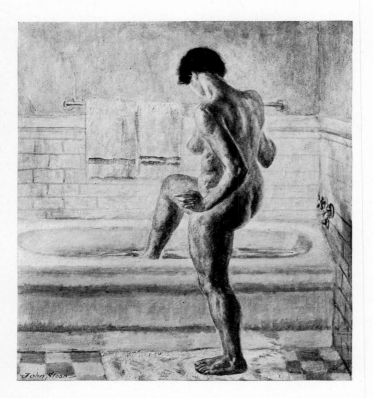

1928—NUDE STEPPING IN
TUB. (Collection of Spencer
Penrose) *The projecting corner
of this figure is well expressed.
The color-textural modelling well
searched out, and I am inclined
to like the design of the canvas
as a whole. Painted directly with
little glazing if any.*

1929—CHARCOAL FIGURE
(Drawing)

1928—SELF PORTRAIT. John
Sargent once defined a portrait as
a picture made from a human head
which had something wrong with
the eyes or the nose or the mouth,
and he surely spoke from experience.
The advantage of self-portraiture lies
in the fact that no heed need be
paid to these defects. Perhaps you
will agree with me that this work
concerns itself with more than visual
representation of shape. Underpainted with some color, top colors
glazed and scumbled.

1929—THE FALL OF THE VIL-
LAGE BASTILLE. The village,
Greenwich, in New York City; the
bastille being demolished was the
ladies' jail and market of the Jefferson Market Court group. The foreground structure is a stairway of the
Sixth Avenue elevated railway. The
site is now occupied by a house of
detention for women, much better
equipped for such purposes.

1929—BILL SHUSTER. This sketch portrait was the product of a duel in paint. Bill and I met in deadly combat in my studio in Santa Fe, and he banged out one of me and I fired this shot at him. Under the circumstances, while no masterpiece, it shows pronounced evidence of right good thinking. The paint is applied in clearly graphic way, the undertones well considered and clinched by the linear coloration of the upper painting.

1929—BILL SHUSTER "SECOND STATE." The second reproduction shows the effect of taking out visual perspective by shortening the near shoulder and slightly enlarging the far one. A comparison of the two will show the increase in realization.

1929—NUDE AND SPANISH JUG.
(Collection of Mrs. Spencer Penrose)
This rich, colorful picture was underpainted in oil monochrome enriched
by subsequent glazings in varnish oil.
Painted with speed and spirit in spite
of the indirect technique.

1929—BLOND NUDE AND FLOW-
ERS. Here again is a rather charming
color-plastic result heavily underpainted
in oil with cobalt drier and glazed two
days later with varnish medium. Notice
how the far leg has been increased in
size and visibility.

1928—NUDE AND REM-
BRANDT. This type of studio
picture often, as in this case, indicates insufficient steam heat for
figure work during the winter. A
good sense of solidity and rich-
ness of color-sculptural quality
are noticeable, at the same time
the softness of the flesh when
compared with the surroundings
is evident. One of the first pictures underpainted with tempera.
Flaxseed emulsion jells in a cool
room, but is fine for impasto.

1929—NUDE ON NAVAJO BLANKET—A very complete panel in which little use is made
of the linear technique except in turning from the light. This is a decided variation from our
general principle which calls for the lines as color-textural definition of the lightened surface.
More visual than some, perhaps. The increase in volume of the far side of the figure is very
successful because quite unnoticeable.

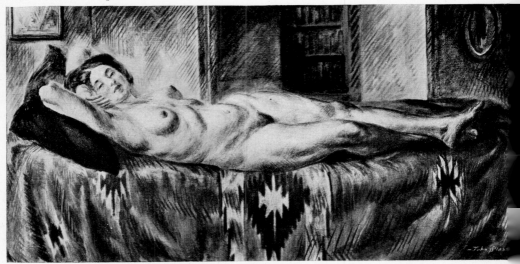

1929—McSORLEY'S CATS. A drawing of this old bar made for Norman Hapgood's 'Harpers Weekly' helped me to produce this painting. It is underpainted and glazed and essays a richer, deeper tone than other McSorley subjects up to this date. The characters at the table, left foreground, are Hippolyte Havel, Art Young, George O. Hamlin, and J. S. Others at the bar were familiar guests of Bill who is engaged in the regular ceremony of feeding the cats at the rickety old refrigerator.

1929—GIRL IN REVERY. *Underpainted in tempera this study of Yosene Kerr, daughter of Balfour Kerr the artist, pleases me. The performance is light and fluent and the color-texture good. A quality of interpretation of a mood is obvious. Note the use of linework in light as well as shade areas.*

1929—NUDE IN A BEDROOM. *This painting made from a slight pencil sketch has undeniable plastic realization; concerns itself with things, not appearances. It affords an interesting study in contrast with "The Cot" of 1907. Note and regret if you will the absence of what might be called emotional quality.*

1930—VAGIS, THE SCULPTOR.
When a news agency asked for a photograph of this picture informing me
that it had been awarded a portrait
prize, I told them there must be some
mistake, that I did not paint portraits.
When they gave me the title of the
picture I remembered that there was
a possibility that it might be so classi-
fied, but that it should be designated,
or shall we say condemned, to a prize
on those grounds was most surprising.
Strong color-textural accompaniment to
volume and graphic vitality.

1930—JUANITA. Charming example
of the pretty girl of an old family in
Santa Fe. The name Roderiguez will
probably be found in the annals of the
Conquistadores. She might properly
have been given more delicacy, but I
was interested more in her vigorous
youth. Writing of this painting from
memory I feel completely satisfied with
it. Faults, if any, are forgotten.

1929—MISCATIONARY. (Collection of Helen Farr) This picture is one of my favorites. It is fine in color and graphically direct in design. The color relations are important, the black and white has nothing to say in this particular. I have an unholy liking for the name—a combination of Miss, cat, and dictionary.

1929—NUDE, FOUR SENSES. This is probably one of the most successful of the studies in form and color-texture differentiation. A student may easily observe the relationship to the technique of tradition by way of Renoir. Like all the nudes much is lost through the vagaries of photographic chromatics.

1930—McSORLEY'S, SATURDAY NIGHT. *Here we have McSorley's during the dark days of prohibition. Had all saloons been conducted with the dignity and decorum of McSorley's, prohibition could never have been brought about. Saloons would not have been closed. McSorley's never was closed. An example of the triumph of right over might. The mugs became smaller, the prices higher, the crowd greater. Painted from blessed memory.*

1930—CHRISTIAN SOLDIERS.
Five devout señoras with the black
fringed shawls proudly escorting the
gold fringed banner of Our Lady.
Procession leaving the Cathedral.

1929—NUDE AND PORTFOLIO
CASE. (Collection of Helen Farr)
A rich toned panel with the light
quality well handled. Evidently
there was no need for any linear
texture, this often is the case where
the lighted areas are rather small.

1930—THE NEW HOMESTEAD.
*A housewarming in the ten by twelve
shack of artist Will Shuster. Some of
the corn liquor is still in the demijohn
in the clothesbasket.*

1930—DOLLY (Drawing)

1933—NUDE AND BREAKFAST TRAY (Etching)

1930—KOSHARE IN THE DUST. A group of dancers who typify the spirits of the ancestors and are mistakenly called clowns. Their bodies, covered with white clay striped with black and earth-red, enveloped in a twister of dust. Painted from memory. Drawing, much less painting is not permitted during the dances.

1931—ROBERT HENRI (*Etching*)

1931—NUDE ON POSING STAND
(*Etching*)

1933—NUDE AT DRESSING TABLE
(*Etching*)

1932—NUDE AND CHIEF BLANKET. *This is an early example of my use of a linear textural super-glaze of color. It has always stood out in my estimation of this period. Broad glazing in color augmented by the super-glazing lines. Lately, I have attempted what might be called greater harshness of color-texture.*

1932—FLOWER BED IN WASHINGTON SQUARE. A flaring bed of cannas and an autumnal coloring in the trees were the inspiration of this painting. Notice the rhythmic relationship between the wriggling tree and the girl on the left. Eight happy years were spent living and working in the studio apartment, center.

1931—NUDE AND BOWL OF FRUIT (Etching)

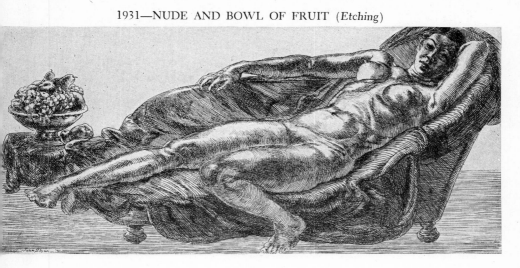

1931—ARACHNE. The sculptural design of this figure seems to me striking and the foreshortened right leg well done. The head would be larger if wishing could change it. In order to create the sensation of a white complexion, I remember avoiding the temptation to force the color-texture with red and orange tones.

1933—NUDE ON NAVAJO BLANKET. (Torso) A curious and striking study of a warm brown torso thrown against the old whites and red and black lozenges of an old blanket. Notice the absence of perspective distortion.

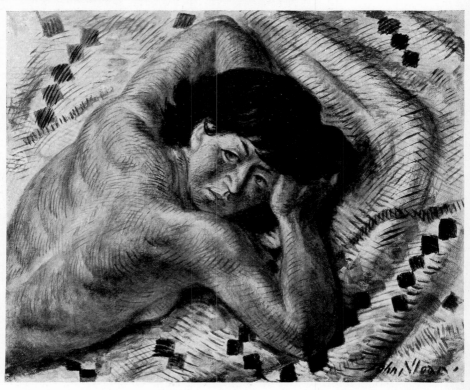

1932—SUSANNA IN SANTA FE. A sun bather utilizing the health giving rays. The spectators are "purely imaginary and not intended to represent any persons living or dead."

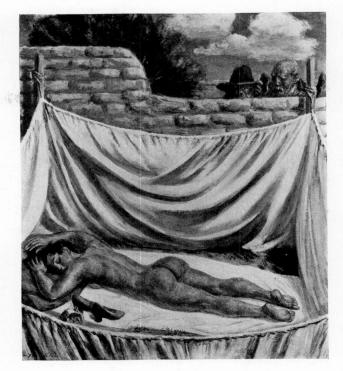

1932—GIRL, BACK TO THE PIANO. An excellent color tonal quality pervades this canvas. The linear texture comes and goes, here and there, and is perhaps on that account very satisfactory. The nature of the light is well expressed. The photo seems to search out the painting more than the eye does.

1932—NUDE ON BLUE COVERED BED.
(Collection of Amelia Elizabeth White) *The
flesh tones with blue coverlet and a yellow,
wooden bed work well together. The structural activity of the figure is right well chosen.*

1932—SCULPTRESS IN RED. *The heavy
impasto of the underpainting being in a gum
tempera gave some trouble. The effect of
the picture is rich and strong and I like it.
Its faults seem good qualities.*

1933—STANDING NUDE
(Etching)

1933—NUDE, TERRA COTTA.
This title indicates my own satis-
faction in the force of color-plastic
statement in this picture. The fact
that it may not look like flesh
to some is a recommendation for
its creative strength.

1933—BILLET-DOUX. (Collection of Amelia Elizabeth White)
Not all of these nudes have emo-
tional content. The fact that this
quality made its appearance in this
canvas led to the title and the
little folded note.

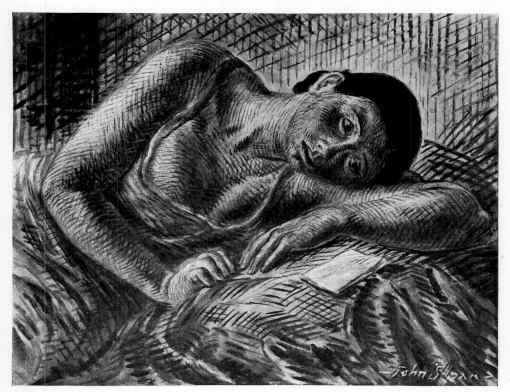

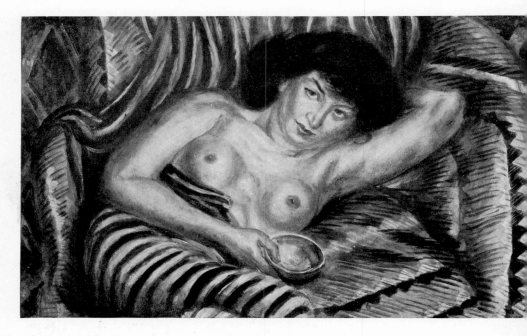

1933—THE BRASS BOWL.
This apparently has more of an
interest in the personality of the
subject than other examples in
this collection. Perhaps I'm wrong
but I think this is largely because the linear identification of
the flesh surfaces is not present,
and did not seem necessary.

1933—BLONDE ON CRIM-
SON CHAISE. As a composi-
tion one might ask for a little
more head and foot room here.
An example of bold application
of the principle of graphic color-
textural statement.

1933—MODEL IN DRESSING ROOM. I am happy about the summer of 1933. It followed a year of enforced idleness. A sense of ripening begins to pervade me. I am sixty-two years old, almost ready to study abroad. Some day I'll grow up and go to Paris and Rome and Amsterdam and Madrid and drink of the fountain of the past. No hurry, though, I still have my ideas to work out. This is a painting that proves I am going somewhere.

1933—NUDE IN HOUSE COAT, MIRROR. (Collection of Dr. Mary Halton) Here we have charm, I believe, a very essential quality for many consumers of art. Like all pictures in which the color has great plastic importance, it is a difficult problem for the photographer.

1934—NAT SMOLIN. The potentialities of what I call a linear glaze in aiding the sense of realization are shown in this portrait. The thing exists as a shape under its color-shell. Few areas of paint are allowed to stand without graphic linear support. Tactile sensation is enhanced. What is desired is more realness than the eye can see.

1933—GITEL WITH LITTLE BOOK. (Collection of Helen Farr) An unusual design, the color is very well textured and brilliant. Notice the resistance of perspective in the arms and hands.

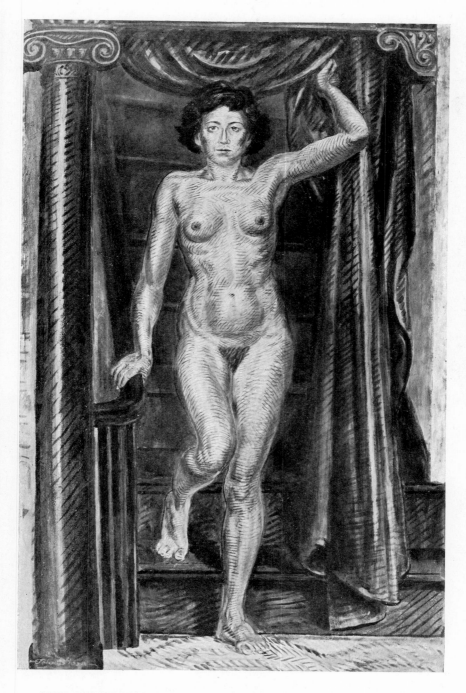

1933—NUDE AT FOOT OF STAIRS. *Asked what he thought of this painting the artist blushed inwardly and confessed that he rated it with anything in the nude line that had been done for a hundred years. We hope our publishing this statement will not be called a breach of confidence.*

1934—BLONDE ON GREEN COVERED CHAIR. *It pleased the artist when this painting was hung in the Museum of Modern Art in a show from which selections were to be made for their exhibition in Paris. Disappointment followed. It was weeded out as being unfit to represent United States art in that art center. They like stronger echoes, perhaps.*

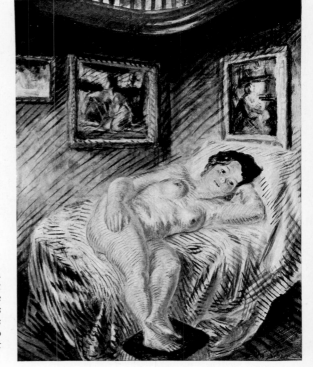

1934—NUDE, COZY CORNER. *The contrast between the clear light on the figure and couch and the shadow under the balcony in this little picture is less abrupt and gives an important quality. The photo makes the change very abrupt. It is a likable picture.*

1934—OLD TAMMANY HALL. (Collection of the Metropolitan Museum of Art) A wicked old edifice, wigwam of the famous political organization which dominated New York for many generations. This brick and gray stone sample of middle 19th century architectural villainy lurked in a kind of sinister half-gloom until it was demolished a few years ago. The cheap gaiety of East 14th Street passed it unheeding.

1934—SEA FOOD. The memoranda sketch for this picture was made, I remember, on a scrap of newspaper. It consisted only of quick drawings of the two stuffed fish upon the wall. So strongly did I feel the resemblance between them and the men taking part in the incident that further portrait memoranda were unnecessary.

1934—NUDE WITH KITTEN AND RIBBON. (Collection of Amelia Elizabeth White) A nude study that turns out to be an attractive composition, vigorous in handling and full in color. This canvas would not come— working from the model. A later attack brought the inventive treatment necessary to solve it.

1933—LOOKING OUT ON WASHINGTON SQUARE. Painted during the only summer that I have spent in New York in the last twenty-seven years. A summer indoors in a big, high-ceilinged studio, which I occupied from 1927 to 1935, overlooking Washington Square and the arch at the end of Fifth Avenue. Children dabbled like ducks in the pool around the fountain almost under my window; the busses picked up hundreds to ride up Riverside Drive, teeming, stewing life below me; coolness, peace, and plenty of work; a memorable summer indoors. A kind of an ivory tower life, despised, as heaven is, by some.

1935—STUDY FOR REALIZATION
seated figure (Drawing)

1935—STUDY FOR REALIZATION
head and shoulders (Drawing)

1935—STUDY FOR REALIZATION *reclining figure* (Drawing)

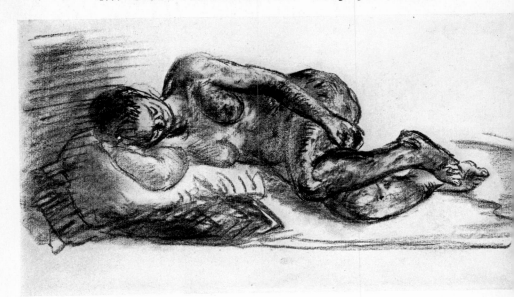

1935—PORTRAIT OF AMELIA ELIZABETH WHITE. (Collection of Amelia Elizabeth White) *My sitter asserts her liking for this picture which to my mind rates her high in ability to look on a picture as a created work. These examples of the linear super-glazing texture are difficult to photograph. I see no reason why a painter should not pride himself on producing pictures which are exclusively themselves.*

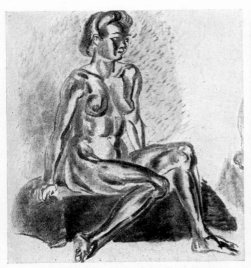

1935—STUDY FOR REALIZATION
seated figure (Drawing)

1938—SEATED ON FLOOR IN KIMONO
(Drawing)

1935—STUDY FOR REALIZATION large recumbent nude (Drawing)

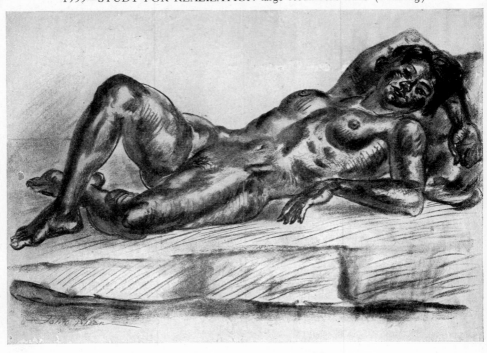

1935—OUR CORNER OF THE STUDIO. The writer and artist frankly admits a strong personal liking for this picture. It is a record of our home life in the studio. The cat on the balustrade is a figment of the imagination. The picture has power, and the problems of chiaroscuro are well met. Its departure from visual representation is much greater than is apparent. It was painted by daylight and from memory in the studio which was the setting.

1936—NUDE ON THE ROOF. This intimate glimpse at life on the skyline of New York is quite a figment of the imagination. The pose took place within the studio. An expert on cats may find some fault; who cares?

1935—NUDE WITH PINK NOTE. (Collection of Philip B. Goetz) In spite of a slight sense of confining space about this figure due to the speed with which many of these nudes are produced, I regard this painting as one of the 'first string'. Take my word, if you will, for the rich and brilliant color. Judge for yourself as to the sculptural significance and the sweeping design.

1936—BLOND NUDE ON FLOOR. *This small picture is a pet of mine. The design is unusual, the color rather gorgeous. Another good thing about it is that not everyone likes it. It's sort of a solved problem child for me.*

1938—MARY REGENSBURG, ARTIST. (Collection of Mrs. Leonard Feist) *A strong, clear blue background is one of the important areas in this portrait. Against this the flesh, dark brown hair, and green gold of the bodice tell quite beautifully. The sitter, now the owner, was a student in my studio for several winters.*

1938—SANTA FE SUNSET. (Collection of Amelia Elizabeth White) *This was what I call a possible sunset. Vivid gold and amber with a remote turquoise sky, seen from Will Shuster's homestead in the foothills six or seven miles west of Santa Fe.*

1936—ROAD UP THE CANYON.
New Mexico's sunny glare and clear
atmosphere are well felt in this
study. The linear textural markings
add greatly to a sense of realization.
Anyone present when these were
first applied to what already seemed
a complete statement, would be convinced of their utility.

1937—BARBARA IN STRIPES.
This small picture reproduces very
well and might on that account help
as a technical example. Monochrome
green and white tempera for face
and arms, three other light tempera
tones understating colors of background, hair, and sweater. Followed
by glazes in varnish oil color. Then
the linear color-texture.

[331]

1937—BETTER MOUSE TRAPS. *Small groups of Indians from Santo Domingo erect these shelters along the Albuquerque highway in hopes that some passing traveller may be tempted to buy their pottery.*

1937—NUDE AND NINE APPLES. *In the Addison Gallery catalogue last year I wrote, "Every good picture leaves the painter eager to start again, unsatisfied, inspired by the rich mine in which he is working; hoping for more energy, more vitality, more time—condemned to painting for life."*

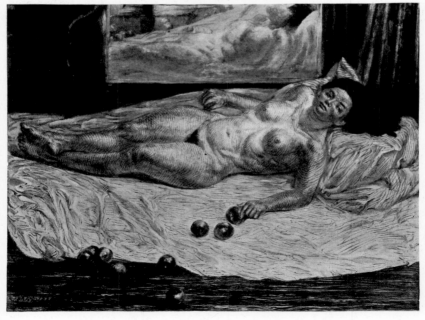

1938—PICNIC, ARROYO HONDO. A happy party taking a holiday lunch to a spot five miles out of town. This dam originally intended as a reservoir, became filled with silt so rapidly that its only function now is erosion control.

1939—STANDING NUDE Red, Yellow and Gray (Drawing)

1939—SHELL OF HELL (Etching)

1939—THE FIRST MAIL ARRIVES AT BRONXVILLE, 1846. (Mural for Procurement Division, U. S. Treasury Department) When I painted two mural panels for a frieze around the lecture room of the Pennsylvania Academy of Fine Arts in Philadelphia in about 1894, I had an idea that I was through with large scale productions; in fact about that time I refused a job painting theatre curtains. Years rolled by for a time, and then they whizzed by, for that's the way they go when you get older. Last year brought a proposal from the Treasury Department that I paint a sixteen foot mural for the Bronxville Post Office. I wondered what work of mine had indicated to them that I could paint a mural, but I replied that I would undertake it. Now it is done and I like it. The photo misses the best of it. It is light in color, not in whiteness. The dominant color chord is red-purple, orange, and blue-green. I have referred to the fore-shortening in train and horse and the side of the house. As you normally look at this page you see it as it looks about thirty feet away. If I were forty years old, I might think of taking up mural painting.

DETAILS FROM MURAL

INDEX

INDEX

imitation of, 49, 83
line and sculpture, 58
local color of, 127
plan in seeing, 100
plastic, 16, 148
projection, 64, 72—74, 78, 101
sculpturing of, 59, 62, 63—65, 77, 159—160
Formalin, 172
Formulae, 38, 46, 49, 50, 58, 62, 88, 110, 115, 163, 179
Freedom, 4
French critics, 32
French art, 22, 28, 34

Gavarni, lithographs, 186
Gelatin, 177
Genius, 8, 36
Geometric design, 70—72
German artists, 112, 164
Gilbert, Douglas, 10
Giorgione, 164
Giotto, 1, 43, 44, 74, 75, 88, 89
Glackens, William, 3, 25, 37, 82
Glackens' technique, 46—48
Glazing (see Form and Color), 136—143, 176—177
Glazing medium, 176
Glue size, 170
Glycerine, 187
Gothic period, 22, 85
Gouache, 88
Government, 4, 5, 28
Government, interest in art, 27—29, 154
Goya, 1, 42, 72, 183, 185
Grammar, 19, 44, 156
Graphic symbols, 53, 109
Graver, use of, 182
Great art, 42, 51, 61, 66
Greco, El, 37, 38, 44, 47, 50, 75, 83, 91, 112, 139
Greek, use of proportion, 90
Grosz, George, 56
Grounds, aquatint, 184—185
Grounds, etching, 180—182
Grounds, gesso, 166, 168—172
Growth, 150
Grünewald, 164
Guys, Constantin, 2

Half-oil ground, 168, 171—172
Harmony (see Composition, Color, etc.)
and contrast, 65, 70
of concept, 49, 76
of light and shade, 62, 80
of relief, 44, 74
of textures, 65
Hals, Frans, 2, 15

Head, the, 13, 90, 92, 94, 95, 105—108
Heights, scale of, 121
Henner, 25
Henri, Robert, 1, 3, 6, 7, 83, 116
Highlights, 55, 60, 107, 139, 145, 161
Hogarth, 2, 20, 58, 81
Hokusai, 84, 111
Holbein, 143
Homer, Winslow, 3
Hues (see color)
Human kindness, 87—88, 106
Humanism, 2, 9, 41, 147,
Humor, 81, 147

Ideograph, 18, 189
Ikons, Russian, 42
Illusions, optical, 68—69
Illustration, 1, 2, 3, 7, 44, 81, 86, 150
Image, 12, 14, 18, 21, 37, 40, 41, 189
Imagination, 14, 18, 37, 97, 99, 146, 189
Imitation, 12, 35—38, 47, 49, 54, 60, 157, 163, 178
Impasto, 113, 172—177
Impossible, painting the, 52
Impressionism, 3, 163
Impulse, 20, 34, 37, 39, 40, 50
Independence of the artist, 33—34, 190
Independent Artists, Society of, 7, 14, 31, 155
Indian, American, 14, 21, 22, 31, 154
Individualism, 22, 34, 35
Individuality, 36
Inferiority complex, 5, 23
Informatory drawings, 85—86
Ingres, 100, 102, 111, 165, 180
Innocuous work, 52
Inspiration, 6, 7, 41
Institution, 29, 30
Interest in life, 39, 42, 45, 79, 146, 165
Inventor, 36, 40, 54, 57
Isolating solution for tempera, 176
Italian art, 22, 100, 125

Japanese, work of, 1, 22, 57, 72, 149
Jewish Bride, by Rembrandt, 114
John Brown's Body, 9
Joyce, James, 36
Juries, art, 30, 33

Keene, Charles (in Punch), 2, 104
Kubota, Beisen, 1

Labor organizations, 34
Laboratory, 8, 192
Landscape, 146—153
Language of art, 6, 14, 36, 40, 156
Leech, John, 2, 58, 79, 81, 178, 180
Leisure, 9, 164

M